IN HIS OWN WORDS

GRAV

IN HIS OWN WORDS

Gomer

Published in 2008 by
Gomer Press, Llandysul, Ceredigion, SA44 4JL

ISBN 978 1 84323 944 4

A CIP record for this title is available from the British Library.

Grav, Lyn Jones and Ray Gravell, was published by Gomer
in 1986. Translations of parts of that autobiography are
included here with the permission of Lyn Jones and the Estate
of Ray Gravell.

This book is published with the financial support of the
Welsh Books Council.

Printed and bound in Wales at
Gomer Press, Llandysul, Ceredigion

To
Mari, Manon and Gwenan

Acknowledgements

The Editor and the Publishers are indebted to the following for every favour and kindness during the compilation and production of this book: Sain Recordiau Cyf, Rhean Harris, Owain Jones, Mark Thomas, Bethan John, Sharon Griffiths, Cari Lewis, Heddyr Gregory, Geraint and Margaret Rowlands, John Hefin and Elin, Dennis Peel, Rob Lewis, Donald Williams, Rachel Nicholson, Les Williams Ferry-side, Wyn and Alun Jones Craig-cefn-parc, Keith Jones and Sian Gwynedd BBC Cymru, Steve Groves and Miles Orchard BBC Wales, Tomos Owen, and Angharad Mair, Tinopolis.

Picture Acknowledgements

Thanks also to the photographers, agencies and individuals for their permission to reproduce the photographs in this book – many refusing to accept payment for their services. In those instances where it was impossible to trace the owners, the Editor and the Publishers urge the relevant individuals to contact Gomer to make sure that their contributions be recognized in any subsequent reprints of *Grav in his own words*.

S4C: viii, 170, 174, 192, 193 (bottom right), 202, 219, 223; South Wales Evening Post: xi, 44, 56, 63, 68, 82, 89, 93, 98, 109, 141, 150, 153, 156, 161, 199, 205, 225, 228, 233, 244, 252, 255; BBC: xii, 66, 72, 168, 208, 210, 212, 217, 218, 232, 238, 253; Alun Morris Jones: 2, 49, 86, 167 (bottom), 178, 185-187, 240-241, 251, 262; the J.J. Williams collection: 4, 111, 112-114, 117, 127, 206; the Gravell family collection: 7, 9, 11, 14, 15, 17, 18, 23, 27, 180, 182, 193 (apart from the bottom right), 249, 257; Ray Wood: 12, 37; John Harris: 24, 88; the Adrian Howells collection: 31; the Les Williams collection: 43; Huw Evans Agency: 47, 51, 158; Tinopolis: 62; Marian Delyth: 65; Colorsport: 84, 124, 133, 136, 138-139, 148; George Herringshaw (Assoc. Sports Photo): 102; the Dafydd Iwan collection: 119; Wyn Jones: 154, 172, 194, 222 (top), 227, 230-231, 254; National Eisteddfod of Wales: 163, 229; David Jones: 197; David Williams: 222 (bottom); Urdd Gobaith Cymru: 248; Gravells Kidwelly: 250; Terry Morris: 264.

Contents

Introduction

Some blamed Grav's uneasiness on the result – Wales, after all, had just lost for the second time in their history at the Stadio Flaminio in Rome and the former centre felt it deeply. Others were less convinced – knowing that he was a slave to his diabetes, they sensed he was suffering the physical pains of that disease. Some eight of us had ordered a meal in the restaurant nearby, but Ray politely made his excuses and said that he didn't feel up to joining us. A few weeks later, our fears were confirmed when the terrible news broke about the condition of the modest man from Mynyddygarreg, and that he was about to face some serious surgery at Glangwili Hospital, Carmarthen.

In a matter of hours, the news spread from one end of the country to the other that Grav had lost his leg. The cards arrived at Brynhyfryd in their thousands from the four corners of the world, and the postman quietly cursed him that a lorry was now needed instead of the usual red van. However, within a few days things were looking up – Ray's positive attitude, the support of his family, and the care and expertise of the medical team meant that the daily broadcaster was recovering quickly and was full of confidence for the future. Weeks later, he was home, communicating with the nation via the radio, visting Morriston Hospital for an artificial limb, and waxing lyrical about the honour of presenting a prize on the stage of the Urdd National Eisteddfod in Carmarthen.

Before long he was wearing his new leg and driving his customized Renault Scenic. Mid-July he was addressing the hundreds that had come to the Stradey Park hotel to greet him, and in August he was kicking off a testimonial match against Bath at Stradey. Come September, Grav was back on air presenting his morning show live from Stradey Park, as the whole nation breathed a collective sigh of relief. Autumn half-term he went on a family holiday to Spain, and there, on October 31st, one of the nation's giants died, a man who had contributed so much in so many areas – on the sportsfield, on the small and silver screens, as Sword Bearer in the National Eisteddfod, and on the Welsh and English airwaves. Some time later, in a television interview, the journalist and travel writer Jan Morris presented a warm tribute to the mountaineer and pioneer Sir Edmund Hillary. She eloquently extolled the great New Zealander's virtues, referring to the way he had succeeded, through courage and actions, to immortalize himself in so many countries, notably his homeland and Nepal. And then, almost instinctively, Jan Morris (who had been *The Times*'s correspondent in 1953 when Hillary and Tensing Norgay reached the summit of Everest) added this post-script: 'The only person I can think of who had the same iconic influence as Hillary would be Wales's Ray Gravell.' Praise indeed!

It was Gomer Press's intention some three years ago to commission Ray to add a sequel to *Grav*, the autobiographical volume published in 1986 and written in conjunction with Lyn Jones. Gomer were keen for Ray to document all those new experiences he had enjoyed since retiring from the rugby field. He agreed, but as with so many others, there were too many projects on the go, and after a year or two, there was very little recorded on paper. However, after some jibing and coaxing, he was persuaded to compose a very interesting essay for *Y Mynydd Hwn* (subsequently *On this Mountain*), and it was an experience that proved most satisfying. Following his surgical treatment, he agreed to record his recent experiences on tape, and the result was a succession of poignant revelations. After his untimely death, Gomer contacted me, and since Mari and the girls were in favour, I began collating all that Ray had written, and listened to dozens of his broadcast tapes to ensure a comprehensive compilation of Grav – in his own words.

I met Grav for the first time at Stradey Park in 1973 in a club match between Llanelli and Ebbw Vale, and found him a giant in the true sense of the word – sometimes creative, sometimes destructive. He was a pastmaster at launching himself at the opposition, a juggernaut of strength and determination. But he could also be balletically stylish as he ran with the ball in two hands before distributing to his wingers with mathematical precision. Over the last quarter of a century, I spent many entertaining hours in his company at rugby grounds all over Europe, and found him a gentle, affable character, a teddy bear indeed – and thousands can testify the same way to his warm and winning personality.

The book is dedicated to John Hefin and Elin, Pinky, Mike 'Bach' Evans, John 'Tremendous' Jenkins, David and Indeg Gravell and the company, Les Williams and family, all the members of Mynyddygarreg RFC, Liz and Wyn Smith, Martin, Nanette and Catrin, Geraint and Siôn and the hard-working crew of *Y Clwb Rygbi*, Huw Evans, Roy Bergiers, Derek Quinnell and Delme Thomas, DH, Aunty Babs, Eamon, Alma and Cillian, Joe and Glenys, Albert Francis, the crew and listeners of *Rhaglen Grav*, Frank Hennessy and the crew of *I'll Show You Mine*, Menna Richards and all the staff of BBC Cymru, Robert and Debbie at WRW, players, administrators and supporters of Llanelli Scarlets, and the people of Wales; but, most of all, to the trio in Brynhyfryd – Mari, Manon and Gwenan.

Alun Wyn Bevan

Launching *Straeon o'r Strade* (later *Stradey Stories*) in the company of Scarlets favourites past and present.

Part 1

From the Mountain
1951–1986

(A selection from *Grav* Lyn Jones and Ray Gravell, Gomer 1986)

Brynhyfryd in Mynyddygarreg.

1

My Father's Dream

I heard the news on the radio. 'This is the team that will represent Wales against France at the Parc des Princes . . .' A dream had come true – a moment I'd imagined and wished for since childhood. My eyes were filled with tears. It was probably the first time I cried tears of joy. But there was one thing missing: there was one person, more than anyone else, that should have been there to share the dream with me; after all, it was his dream in the first place, until he passed it on to me. Dad's dream. I'm sure that every father can imagine his son running onto the fresh green turf of the National Stadium wearing the red shirt, and it was the same for my father. Sadly for me, he didn't live to see it realised, but I'll always remember his help in the early days, when a muddy field in Mynyddygarreg was my rugby pitch.

I was one of six new caps wearing the red shirt for the first time in a full international match for Wales; the year was 1975, and the date, January 18th, has been forever ingrained in my mind. At last, I had the chance to represent my country. I was in a state of complete euphoria, and couldn't fathom the reality of the situation for a few days, but reading the papers brought me back down to earth. I was on top of the world, though our chances were slim, according to the pundits.

My first cap in Paris 1975. The team is obeying the photographer's instructions whilst I glance around to see if I can spot some of the Mynyddygarreg faithful arriving. Six new caps: Graham, myself, Trevor, Charlie a Steve in the back row and the late John Bevan seated between JJ and JPR.

Everybody who knows me will tell you that I'm an emotional person, and as I struggled to build up some confidence, the days before the Paris match became unbearably tense. Would I play well? Would I manage to create an impression, even if we lost? But I knew that my greatest hour had arrived. The doubts only lasted for a few short seconds and nothing was going to stop me from wearing the red shirt.

Things went surprisingly well in the final trial, and during an early dinner at the Angel Hotel, the chairman of the selectors, Cliff Jones, announced that the team would be named that evening. Some stayed for the announcement, but I headed back west. I was listening to the radio in the car, and as I approached Idole primary school, a voice on the radio named the team that would face the French. I listened carefully as they ran through the list: JPR, JJ, Steve Fenwick, and Ray Gravell – and when I heard my name, I completely lost control of my little green car. To be honest, I didn't hear the names of the others in the team!

I'd heard the announcement, but as an insecure Gwendraeth valley boy, I couldn't believe it. During the previous two seasons, I'd been given the opportunity to play against players such as Gareth and Gerald, and suddenly my name was on the same list as those giants. My little brain found it difficult to absorb the information, despite reading the team's names over and over in the *Sunday Express* the next morning. On Monday, I got up at six to go to work at the Electricity Board in Llanelli, and was warmly congratulated by my colleagues. Shortly after arriving at work, the *Western Mail* reporter was looking for me, and I had to give countless television and radio interviews. Interestingly, I only realised after reading the *Western Mail* that, not only were there six new caps in the team, but also a new captain and coach, namely Mervyn Davies and John Dawes. Before that morning, the sum of my media experience was nothing more than one interview on *Byd y Bêl*. I remember the occasion clearly: it was the first Saturday I played for Llanelli at Stradey, and the last afternoon that D. Ken Jones played for Cardiff before retiring from the game. But during the week before the match, a microphone seemed to be constantly under my nose!

Mam was like a queen that week, dealing with neighbours calling over to congratulate me and answering phone calls, as well as sorting out cards and letters, many of which were from teachers at Carmarthen Grammar School and Burry Port Comprehensive, as well as from countless friends. Those cards are still kept safely in a box at home.

A few celebrations were held at the Greenfield and Greenale pubs in Mynyddygarreg that week. We certainly knocked back a pint or two! As it was my first cap, I couldn't play for Llanelli the following Saturday, but I went to Monday night's training session, and the first two who came to see me were two very important people in my career, two who had been predicting for over a year that I would play for Wales. Bert Peel, the Llanelli 'physio', was the first to congratulate me, with the gracious Carwyn James not far behind. I can still hear his words clearly today; in his tenor voice he said, 'You've been chosen because of the way you've played for Llanelli throughout the season. Make sure that you play your own game.' Those words of advice were indispensable, and helped to ease the nagging uncertainty in my mind.

The official card from the Welsh Rugby Union arrived to confirm that I'd been chosen, as well as an official letter with the travel itinerary. I was asked to bring a black suit for the official dinner. Slowly, it was all beginning to sink in, although my head was still in the clouds as I packed on Wednesday night to travel to Cardiff on Thursday, where we'd meet for a training session at the Arms Park. I travelled from Ferryside to Cardiff with Derek Quinnell and Phil Bennett – I didn't know the way to Cardiff back then!

I arrived at the Arms Park, the training went well, and a team of students from Cardiff College of Education played against us for about an hour. We then headed back to the Angel Hotel, and were all taken after dinner to a cinema in Cardiff; afterwards, it was back to the hotel and straight to bed. J. J. Williams shared a room with me for the weekend, and unfortunately for him, I didn't sleep, and as a consequence, poor JJ didn't have much sleep either. My mind was racing, I kept tossing and turning, and I spent most of the evening asking questions to JJ and smoking my Woodbines non-stop. It was a terribly long night, and fair play to JJ for being so patient with me. He didn't complain all weekend, though he's complained many times since then! After breakfast, we got our things together and travelled to Rhoose airport. There, we were confronted by crowds of supporters, all looking forward to a weekend in Paris, and eager to share their opinions and advice.

For the first time ever, I saw the romantic city of Paris! We landed at Orly airport and were amazed by the city's sights as we headed for the Terminus hotel in a luxury coach, led by a convoy of policemen on motorbikes. We got to the hotel, where we were welcomed by Myrddin, Peter and Tal from Mynyddygarreg. A wave of *hiraeth* hit me when I saw them. Thankfully, JJ looked after me and found our room key and led the way to the lift and down the corridors; then back down to the dining room for lunch, where John Dawes had ensured that Steve Fenwick and I were sitting together. He wanted John Bevan (whose services to the game were lost when he passed away at a young age), Steve and I – the three new players in midfield – to have a chance to discuss our responsibilities. John Dawes advised us to be very physical against Dourthe and Bertranne; at the same time, he gave us free rein to play the game in our own way. Psychologically, his advice was a great boost – it was wonderful to know that our coach wanted us to play to our strengths, and not be tied down by strict tactics.

After lunch, small groups of us went to see the sights of the city. We gazed in amazement at extravagant shop windows and inhaled the distinctive French air – a mixture of garlic and coffee and a touch of *Gitanes*. I still wasn't convinced that it wasn't a dream – but when I saw a few groups of people dotted around the streets in red-and-white caps, I realized that it *was* happening to me. Back in

The photograph that adorned the newspapers following the announcement of the Welsh team versus France in January 1975.

the hotel at the end of the afternoon, we met a few supporters who were all looking for tickets to the match. I was bowled over by their enthusiasm – they'd travelled all the way in good faith that they'd find a ticket somewhere. After a meal, we were taken to the *Folies Bergères* – what a place! – I'd heard about it before, but never thought that I'd have a chance to visit! It was totally unbelievable: we went into an enormous hall and could do nothing but stare, open-mouthed, at the spectacle. Naked women were entering the stage from all directions, from the ceiling, the sides, everywhere – hell, a man didn't know where to look next! I had enough on my mind without having to deal with naked breasts all over the place!

At eleven o'clock on Saturday morning, the players went to the captain's room for a team meeting and the coach's final words of advice. It was here that John Dawes always finished his sermon, rather than the changing room. I don't remember a word of what was said in that meeting, apart from the fact that Mervyn Davies's room was full of smoke – and that I was to blame for most of it! Then everyone moved on to the dining room, and I played with the fish on my plate, but couldn't eat a morsel. Finally, we picked up our kit and stepped on the bus that took us to Parc des Princes – Wales's second appearance at the ground. The journey was truly memorable, with a row of policemen on motorbikes leading the way with sirens blaring, and the whole procession moving at a frightening speed through Paris with nothing to stop us, just like a presidential convoy through the city. It was worth playing in France, if only for the thrill of that amazing journey.

I was there, I had arrived, and after leaving my bag in the corner, I went out with the others to walk on the pitch. It was reasonably empty and quiet at that time; no one was standing, by the way, as the pitch was totally surrounded by seats, with plenty of room for everyone. Standing in the middle of the field, I was overwhelmed by its hugeness. Back in the changing room, Mervyn insisted that we got changed, as we had to be ready at least fifteen minutes before the kick-off. On a table in the middle of the changing room, there was a big pile of cards and telegrams. One was from Mam. It knocked me for six. I was thinking about everything now, thinking about Dad and how he would have felt. He would have been there, without doubt, if he were alive – everything was racing through my mind as I read the message. I'd bought Mam a cat called Twdls, and as far as I know, this was the first telegram co-written by a mother and a cat. The message was in English, as it was my mother's first language:

> Dear Raymond,
> All our love.
> Mami and Twdls.

If I was filling up earlier, tears were now streaming uncontrollably down my cheeks. The next thing I remember is someone's hand on my shoulder – Clive Rowlands was there, an emotional person like myself, his eyes also filled with tears after reading the message.

Had some of the French players seen me at that moment, they certainly would have thought that a great big baby in a red shirt was in the centre against them. But truth be told, a wonderful feeling of pride was also surging through my veins the moment I read the message. I'm sure that any psychiatrist would find it difficult to explain how a message from a little cat could turn someone into a bit of a lion! But to me, it was like a direct line to home, and no one on earth could persuade me that my father wasn't near me that afternoon. Afterwards, everyone apart from the team went out of the room and Mervyn, as captain, gave us the final sermon before the match, and reminded everyone, as if I needed reminding, that we were representing Wales. We left the changing room and walked along a corridor until we reached the opening of the tunnel. We had to wait for a while, with both teams standing in parallel rows. The atmosphere was electrifying. Wales in red in one row, the French in white alongside us, and both teams trying to avoid each other's gaze. My mouth felt completely dry, and

One of the Brynhyfryd cats – not Twdls this time but Shamrock yr Ail ('the Second').

my heart was beating like a drum. I don't know which Frenchman was stood next to me, but I became so excited when the band began playing that I gave him a hard (but harmless) punch.

It was time to go onto the field, where the mood had been building up to a climax over the past hour: the loud noise was painful to my ears – cheering, fireworks exploding around the place and a jazz band from Dax playing in the background. When the French team came out, the noise reached a deafening level, and amongst all of this there were about half a dozen cockerels running and hovering around the pitch. The French looked so big and fit and handsome in their white shirts!

The crowd became silent for a few seconds. Suddenly, the band played '*Hen Wlad fy Nhadau*' as I stood in a small circle with my co-players singing – or rather, yelling the anthem as loud as I could, with tears streaming down my face. Gareth Edwards stood next to me, and as he told me many times later, some of my emotion rubbed off on him at that moment. Each word of the anthem had a special significance – it meant everything to me.

At that moment, it was fantastic to be a Welshman.

2

The Boy from the Mountain

September 12th 1951 was a very important date at 36 Station Road, Kidwelly, as it was the day when Raymond William Gravell came into the world. I should add that September 10th of the same year was also important. On this day, two days before my birth, Thomas John Gravell and Nina Eileen John got married – my Mam and Dad! They certainly left things till the last minute!

Dad was born and raised in the village of Mynyddygarreg, the third of four children, with two elder sisters called Eileen and Olive and a younger sister called Barbara. When he was fourteen years old, Thomas John had to start working at the limestone quarry in Mynyddygarreg, about half a mile from the family home, Tan-yr-Heol. Some time later, he began working at the coal mine, which employed most men from the village. Tan-yr-Heol was a small one-storey cottage, with a bedroom and a small kitchen, separated by a pantry cupboard, a long garden behind the cottage, and of course, a toilet at the bottom of the garden. In those days, and to a lesser extent today, Mynyddygarreg was a set of cottages for limestone quarrymen – whoever named it 'Mynydd' ('Mountain') must have had delusions of grandeur, as it is no more than a hillock of limestone, rising around seven or eight hundred feet above Carmarthen Bay. But everyone has a right to dream – even the smallest villages!

Resembling a tight-head prop, here I am on my first birthday.

Ray Wood's photograph from *On This Mountain* – Kidwelly Castle and Carmarthen Bay from Brynhyfryd's patio.

The village of Mynyddygarreg looks down upon the estuaries of the Gwendraeth Fach and the Gwendraeth Fawr. It stands on top of a limestone seam that pushes itself out of the Bay and extends into a rugged ridge between both rivers, passing through Meinciau, Crwbin and Llyn Llech Owain before reaching the Black Mountain. This was my father's habitat, as well as mine. Below stands Trimsaran, facing the sea, alongside the village of Llan-saint, and the town where my mother was brought up – Kidwelly. Dad was a rugby player and a strapping man, over six foot tall, who initially played in Kidwelly's front row. My parents met in a dance after a match – she was a trained hairdresser and had spent the war years with the Wrens in Portsmouth, but was now working in a factory in Llanelli making glasses. And on September 10th, 1951, at Llanelli Registry Office, they were married – and I was one of their wedding gifts! One of their first tasks was naming the flame-haired newborn, but that wasn't a big problem as William was the name of my grandfather on my father's side, and my maternal grandfather was called Robert. There's quite a funny story behind the name Raymond. When my father was born, my grandparents decided to call him Raymond, and William Henry Gravell, my grandfather (Tad-cu to me), was instructed by Gladys, my grandmother, to travel to the registry office to register him as Raymond. Unfortunately, Tad-cu called into the Greenale and Greenfield on his way, to wet the baby's head. When he reached the registry office, he decided to name my father Thomas John, after his brother! I never learned how Mam-gu reacted when she found out! But at least I was given the name that was meant for my father, and soon after September 12th I was christened Raymond William Robert Gravell. But everyone called me Raymond.

For the first three months of my life, I kept everyone awake at Station Road, Kidwelly, before my father persuaded Mam to leave her home in Kidwelly to set up a family home for us three in Bwlch-y-Mynydd, a small, unremarkable cottage, about a mile from the village of Mynyddygarreg towards Pedair Heol.

My father felt discontented in Kidwelly and had been yearning to move back from the town centre to the mountain. The ruins of the cottage are still there today. It was one of the original limestone quarry cottages, with one bedroom, a kitchen and a large open fire – with a lavatory at the bottom of the garden. I have many childhood memories of Henry Hall, the old man who lived on his own in the cottage next door. He re-christened me 'Redman'. Old Henry was a Welsh speaker and he became a close friend of the family. From what I remember, he used to wear a black hat with a wide brim and a heavy coat all year round, and he always had a pipe in his mouth. Dad loved living in Bwlch y Mynydd, as there was plenty of space for him to keep a goat, for milk, and some hens for eggs, and I was raised on goat's milk, which could account for the strength in this body of mine.

To top it all, he could also indulge in one of his favourite pastimes, which was hunting and breeding goldfinches. Being with these animals was one of his greatest pleasures in life – he was very close to nature. What a strange world we live in! Dad worked in complete darkness to earn his living – crouched down in the narrow warrens of Pentre-mawr colliery, Pontyberem. I know that this has been said many times before, but there were long periods of time in winter when Dad went underground before sunrise and came up at the end of a shift when the sun had gone down; but he spent every minute of his spare time with animals, or tending to his garden! He would have been lost without his garden.

Mam made the most of her hairdressing training, and local women would often come over to the cottage in the afternoon to have their hair done. I'll never forget one afternoon in particular, when I had measles and had to stay at home, and Mam was giving a perm to a lady – I was as sick as a dog after inhaling the fumes of the setting lotion. To this day, I still remember that stench, and it still turns my stomach! What with the hairdressing, looking after Dad, and the new screeching baby, Mam's life was busy as well. But the experience of moving from Kidwelly to Mynyddygarreg had been heart-wrenching for her, as she didn't

Nina Gravell (Mam) with the Wrens in Portsmouth.

want to leave the town, and I faced a similar upheaval later in life. But the three of us stayed there, in Bwlch-y-Mynydd, until I was around three years old, when the Council began building a few council houses in the village, for which Dad was put on the waiting list. Suddenly, the queen was given her palace – a brand new council house – on the Heol Gwelfor estate. It was number five, with all the mod cons. Not only did we have running water from a tap in the house, we also had hot water and a flushing toilet, and a bathroom. It was a whole new world. But my father had to sacrifice a few things: the goats and hens had to go, but the goldfinches were kept, and he also had a garden. Most houses at Heol Gwelfor had front gardens with neat green lawns – but not Number Five. We had several carefully planned furrows of potatoes, peas and beans, which yielded good crops.

When I was four years old in the September of 1955, I began my academic career at Mynyddygarreg. I must have been inconsolable on the first day as I still remember the tears and sadness. But I also remember being lifted onto Miss Jones's lap, and the poor teacher trying to comfort me – a screeching little redhead – and convince me that it would be worth returning to school the following day. She must have succeeded in persuading me, as I enjoyed my time at primary school, and I have fond memories of the place.

But there was one constant fear in my life: for some reason, I always dreaded waiting for the work bus to arrive every afternoon. The school bell rang at three o'clock and the Gravells Kidwelly bus brought the workers back from Pentre-mawr to Mynyddygarreg at quarter past three. Every afternoon, one little boy waited, impatiently, for that green one-storey bus to stop at the square. When it arrived, the tall upright figure of Jack Gravell would come into view, stepping down from the bus, with his heavy boots tap-tapping the pavement. As soon as I'd see him safely back from work, I'd run a few hundred yards to get home before him to announce that the man of the house was on his way. Some afternoons

Looking angelic, but it is me, honest!

when I couldn't see him coming off the bus, I remember the fear and panic of thinking that something had happened at work. But then I'd realise that my father, like everyone else from time to time, had taken an opportunity to stay on and work a doubler – which meant working two shifts with no break in between. But the tapping sound of those steel-tipped boots was music to the ears of a five-year-old boy at the end of the afternoon. Dad used to buy those boots from a seller who owned a shoe stall for many years by the clock tower in Carmarthen, in the old market. Going to the stall meant having a trip to town on an Eynon's Trimsaran bus on a Wednesday afternoon, which was a real treat for me – Dad smartly dressed, and carrying a pair of boots in his bag, which would be fitted with new steel tips. Then, the highlight of the day for me – eating a bellyful of faggots and peas from one of the other market stalls. It was a day unlike any other; Dad would be wearing his best clothes instead of his work clothes. For work, he usually wore a flat cap turned sideways on his head and a heavy black coat; there'd be a wooden block under his arm for firewood, and a lunchbox poking out from under the other arm – and some chewing tobacco in his mouth. Sons always want to emulate their fathers, and I was no different and tried to copy everything that Dad did: he smoked and I wanted to smoke; he also chewed tobacco, and I'll never forget the experience of chewing two fingers of Franklin's Shag, when I was only six years old! I never tried to do that again!

I used to look forward to having milk every school playtime, and the experience of eating school dinners was wonderful for a boy who'd never eaten with more than three people round the table. For me, like all children, Christmas at Mynyddygarreg was a very special time – and one of the first presents I can remember having from Father Christmas (or Santa, as we called him) was a wooden horse. At the time, I was very concerned about one thing – and I always discussed it in public, much to my family's embarrassment – and that thing was, could the horse shit? I don't remember this question being answered either way! One thing is for sure, whether or not the horse was real, it was good enough for me to spend endless hours on its back. I dreamt many times that this little Welshman on a wooden horse could defeat everyone who got in his way in the Wild West. For me, there never was a better horse – and it had two handles for ears. Giving free rein to my imagination, I also had a Davy Crockett suit from Santa. One of the most memorable songs of the period was a tribute song to that adventurous pioneer, and every Saturday morning on the radio, the record was played on the programme *Children's Favourites*. Being slightly naïve, I was totally convinced that Mam was sending the request in, every time.

After a year or two, I was old enough to sit with Dad for hours, watching his attempts to catch the wild goldfinches. First, he'd place a tame finch in a cage in the garden hedge, which would attract the wild ones with its twittering. Dad would then breed the birds and treat them with remarkable tenderness, considering that he was such a strong, powerful man.

In time, I was allowed to help with his daily chore of cleaning and feeding the birds, which made me feel like a real man. Some Saturday afternoons, my father wouldn't be around, and I didn't understand this until I found out that he played rugby, for Pontyberem by that time. If he worked the morning shift, he'd often come up from Pentre-mawr pit and head straight for the Pelican pub in Pontyberem (which is the rugby club today) to meet the team, without even washing the coal dust from his hands and face. He was selected to play for the West Wales Union, but unfortunately he broke his shoulder in that game, which meant that his rugby career came to an end soon afterwards. Many of his friends played for Pontyberem, and also worked with him at Pentre-mawr, and they had an extraordinarily close relationship. Perhaps it was partly due to the danger hanging over them like a dark cloud every day, as well as their camaraderie on the rugby field.

For many years, I'd watch my father leaving the house, a double-barrel gun under his arm, a ferret in his sack, and with a smile on his face as he went out

Meeting Santa Claus in Carmarthen market – a little wary of the bearded man.

Pontyberem RFC 1950-51. Jac Gravell
(Dad) fifth from the right in the back row.

hunting. I'd try to persuade him to let me join him so that I'd get to hold the gun; but I wasn't allowed to touch the barrel until I was ten years old.

Back in school, I don't remember football being played at all. If someone brought a soccer ball to school, we'd instinctively pick up the ball and run with it. Everyone at home saw rugby as a natural part of life: Dad played, as did Ron, Mam's brother, who was a full-back for Kidwelly – and when my uncle Ron gave me a pair of rugby boots for my first birthday, before I could even walk, it was quite obvious what the men of the family expected of me! My uncle Ron and Dad were good friends for years, long before my parents met each other. Their conversation would often turn to the exploits of the Stradey boys, the Welsh team, and of course, my father's heroes – men such as Cliff Morgan,

Bleddyn Williams and R. H. Williams. Thanks to the radio, I was introduced to the game at an early age, as I heard the voices of G. V. Wynne Jones, Gilbert Bennett and Alun Williams commentating in English on matches every Saturday afternoon. This, as well as the post-match analysis and discussion, definitely contributed to my passion for rugby, although I wasn't aware of it at the time.

I clearly remember that a new rugby ball would arrive every Christmas. In those days, the ball was shaped more like a balloon than the modern oval ball, and we as children would happily play with it in the street. But after a few seasons, we developed our own stadium – Cae'r Post, Mynyddygarreg – which was the field behind the Post Office. This was our Stradey Park or Arms Park, as the mood took us. It was here that I represented Wales for the first time, and we had to have two teams to make the game interesting. I don't remember representing anyone other than Wales, and sure enough, Wales never lost on Cae'r Post! If it looked as if we were about to be beaten by anyone else, I'd suddenly hear a call for lunch or bedtime! That was convenient, as the field itself was behind the Heol Gwelfor council houses. If we weren't playing an important match on Cae'r Post, the mountain with its tall bracken was ideal for playing Cowboys and Indians, and we'd build dens on the limestone ridges above the school. But at some point during the day, we were inevitably drawn to Cae'r Post for a game of cricket or rugby. Those days, the older boys would also play there, and I'd often get in their way. But as the years wore on, they started to tolerate me. I remember watching boys like Terry Roberts, Eirwyn, John Roberts, John Llechdwni, Mike and Wyndham Morgan the Post, and trying to join in with them. One evening, as it was starting to get dark, Wyndham the Post borrowed my rugby ball for his game. I wanted to go home but I knew that I'd have a row from Dad if I went home without the ball. But he knew very well that the ball would come home safely with me.

Wyndham was a great hero of mine at the time. Wherever I stood in my house, I could always hear the sound of Wyndham's feet striking the leather ball, and as soon as I heard it, I'd be out like a shot to Cae'r Post. Wyndham never played for Wales or the Lions – not even for Llanelli – but for me at the time he represented all that was good about the game, and he regularly played for clubs in the West Wales League, such as Kidwelly, Carmarthen and Pontyberem. Gordon Lewis's parents lived in the same street as us: I hardly ever saw Gordon but always mentioned his name with awe – after all, wasn't he the big star who had played centre for Swansea before moving to Leigh to play Rugby League?

One of Mynyddygarreg's most important institutions was the Brass Band, conducted by D. T. Gravelle, and which was famous across Wales. Every boy and girl in the village usually joined the band; I was no exception, and became a member when I was about eleven years old. My hero Wyndham was already a prominent band member, he and his father, Jim, both featuring on trombone. Some years later, it was a thrill to hear Wyndham win the instrumental solo at the National Eisteddfod.

D.T. was our Malcolm Sargent, and I remember having to learn notes and scales under his eagle eye. But I didn't have the talent or enthusiasm to stay in the band for long, although I enjoyed my time there with my cornet. There were interesting characters there too: D. T. himself, a conductor and deacon, Hywel Morgan, and Dai Davies, father of the singer Janet Rees Davies. Dai worked with my father and the poor man suffered from silicosis, and had to climb quite a steep hill to reach the band's practice shed. I can see Dai now – walking ten yards, leaning against the wall to take his breath for a while, then soldiering on for another ten yards, before stopping again. His whole journey to the bandroom was a series of stop-starts. That's when I became aware of the physical consequences of working underground – taking a breath, walking, stopping and choking. It still amazes me that someone like Dai could summon enough force from his lungs to blow a brass instrument, but scenes like that brought home the painful reality of life to us boys, as we gathered outside the Post Office. I got to know Dai well, as it was my job to take our saw to be sharpened by him.

I started attending Sunday School (not by choice!) at Horeb Methodist chapel. The preacher was the Reverend Gwyn Davies Jones, but my Sunday School teacher was Beynon Glanhiraeth, a highly-respected local farmer. During the hay harvest, many people from the area would lend a hand at Glanhiraeth, and I remember going there with my father. My job was binding the hay, and I always wanted to stay for supper at the end of the day. It was just like a feast in an old mansion house of yore – eating meats and bread, and having a sly sip of ale from the jug. The men went from one farm to another to help, and during school holidays, I followed my father to Gwenllian Farm and Pen-y-groes Farm.

During those summers, the only beaches I saw were Ferryside or Saint Ishmael, and of course, we usually walked from Mynyddygarreg. But one year, I went on holiday all the way to Capel Hendre, near Ammanford – to stay with Eileen and Hedley, Dad's sister and brother-in-law, and to me, it felt like going to the end of the earth. Although I had a warm welcome, I spent most of the week asking to go home. We went for a day trip to Porthcawl in Uncle Ron's car – which was a blue Anglia – and for a long time afterwards I was often reminded that I asked, long before reaching Porthcawl, when I'd be allowed to go home! I didn't want to leave Mynyddygarreg, and to this day, I'm not a good traveller.

Back in school, Hefin Evans, the headmaster, retired, and was succeeded by Hywel Gravelle – another close friend of my father who was also a sports teacher. The first Sports Day between the schools of Kidwelly, Ferryside and Mynyddygarreg was held during those years, and I won the eighty-yard race at Kidwelly park. I also remember playing cricket for the school against Kidwelly on a proper cricket field – instead of the rugged terrain of Cae'r Post! In those days, the attitude of both parents and the public towards teachers was entirely different from that of today. There was an immense feeling of respect towards teachers and their work. Although Hywel and Dad were friends, my father always called him Mr Gravelle in front of me, and that had a big influence on me. It was just common courtesy, perhaps, but it's something I still feel very strongly about.

At the beginning of the 1960s, the boy from Mynyddygarreg had to face the trauma of the dreaded Eleven Plus. When the result came, my marks weren't high enough for me to attend the Gram in Carmarthen. Many of my best friends were going there, but I had to settle for Burry Port Secondary School. That was probably my first big disappointment, and the salty taste of tears still reminds me sometimes of that setback. Everyone tried to convince me that I'd have the opportunity to sit the Thirteen Plus, but the age of thirteen seemed ages away at that point.

By now, the three of us had left our council house, and had been living in Brynhyfryd cottage for three years. Dad felt that he needed the freedom of the mountain top. The cottage was freehold property: a cottage with a bank in front of it, and over the years, the bank became known as Raymond's bank (with a different meaning to that of Lloyds Bank, believe me!) Once again, moving was very upsetting for Mam, as she was very happy in Heol Gwelfor, but this was an opportunity to rent a house before buying it. It was an ideal place for Dad: plenty of space to keep animals and hens, and with the mountain almost on our doorstep, he could go hunting with Mac the spaniel.

I'd say that hunting was a kind of drug for my father – it made him feel contented and at ease with himself. He was very interested in guns. Every time we went to Carmarthen, he'd pop into Jackie Dark – the gunsmith's shop – to look at the guns. I once asked whether I could fire the gun, and was promised that I'd be allowed to do it when I was ten. After waiting for what seemed like a lifetime, my chance came. Dad stuffed soft padding into my coat, and explained to me how the gun worked. We then went out on the mountain with Mac, who began poking his head through the thorns and brambles. Suddenly, his tail wagged excitedly, and Dad explained to me that the dog had nosed a rabbit and that it would probably come out of the brambles across the bank. I soon learned that Dad had a kind of sixth sense as far as animals were concerned; he had a deep understanding of them, which still astounded me years later. Mac pushed the rabbit and it sprung out, exactly as Dad had predicted. I heard a voice shouting, I shut my eyes and fired the gun – I felt a blow on my shoulder, smelled the stench of the cartridge, and heard bells ringing in my head. I opened my eyes and saw Dad, smiling broadly, lifting the rabbit up high – I'd joined the hunt! This was the beginning of something special, which gave me great pleasure for years and also maintained my sense of belonging to Mynyddygarreg. By now, I've come to realise that I must always live near that mountain; I have to be able to smell the bracken.

From then onwards, Dad and I would often go out early together on Saturday mornings to hunt. It always surprised me that Dad was totally opposed to hunting on Sundays. He wasn't an ardent chapel-goer – I have no recollection of him ever going to chapel – but when I'd try to persuade him to come hunting, he'd always flatly refuse. With time, I developed quite a good aim with the gun, and was often given the responsibility of looking after it. Dad could then concentrate on his main interest – ferrets. Behind the house at Brynhyfryd there were a few lime kilns which had become ruins. Dad made the most of their shape and structure, and turned one of them into a chicken shed. Another kiln became a home for the ferrets, as well as a collection of tame pigeons and a few goats. Life was good, and those childhood days were blissful.

Sadly, this chapter of my life in Mynyddygarreg was nearly over. But I wasn't entirely ready to uproot: a few days before the end of the summer holiday and the beginning of the new term, a group of boys, including myself, tried to squeeze into the kiosk by the Post Office. In the crush that ensued, my arm was torn on a piece of glass in a broken window. Blood was gushing out and, in a panic, I rushed to the Post

With Mam and Dad at Christmas – seven years old and less suspicious of Santa by now!

Office, where poor Maggie struggled to stop herself from fainting while phoning the doctor. And instead of beginning the new term in a new school, I had to sit for a week in Brynhyfryd, idly counting the stitches in my wrist. I'm sure that this was the beginning of my habit of always turning up slightly late!

An outside break against the old enemy – Neath.

3

History Lessons

From the beginning, I was raised in a bilingual environment. I'm very aware of the fact that many parents today worry about sending their children to Welsh-medium schools because one or both parents are non-Welsh speakers, but I don't see this as a problem and I can't for the life of me understand their anxiety. My mother was raised in completely English surroundings, but my father was Welsh through and through – a quiet, unaffected Welshman. Mam and I spoke English to each other. We never had a language problem as such. When I was a child, the education system, to all intents and purposes, was an English system which had to be adhered to. But by now, we have progressed to a situation where every child can be educated through the medium of Welsh.

There wasn't a 'Welsh' school that I could attend at that time, and after failing to reach the required standard for Carmarthen Grammar School, I was sent to the Secondary School at Burry Port, hoping for a second chance when I turned thirteen. Although Dad was disappointed by my failure, he set his sights on an apprenticeship for me, either as a carpenter or a mechanic, when I left school.

In September 1963, I found myself on the bus joining the other six from the same primary-school class. I wore a school uniform: black blazer, grey shirt, grey trousers, red-and-black tie and a black cap with a peak. And the fear! I remember the fear that morning just as I remember the fear on my first day at primary school. But I wasn't going to cry in front of everyone at Burry Port!

One of the first people who helped to dispel my fear that week was Peter Leyton, a little English boy who'd moved to Pedair Heol with his family. That first morning, I walked down Wern Terrace at ten past eight with Peter to catch the Eynon's bus, and arrived at school where I was promptly led to assembly. Being in a hall with almost five hundred children, and every teacher up on the stage, was an overwhelming new experience for me.

I was then introduced to my class – 1A, and in that year two teachers had a great influence on me: Ceri Rosser, the Biology teacher, and Alwyn Nolan, the PE teacher. Alwyn was the person who introduced me to the real game of rugby, despite the fact that I'd been playing the game for years on Cae'r Post and had been taken several times by my father to Stradey Park.

I soon realised that woodwork wasn't a subject that appealed to me: I was a right-handed craftsman with two left hands, and it became obvious after a few lessons that I wouldn't be very successful in that field. On the other hand, I enjoyed biology lessons – I suppose it was because of my keen interest in animals and nature from an early age. On top of that, Ceri Rosser was quite a remarkable teacher, and the pupil-teacher relationship developed into friendship years later, partly because he was very interested in rugby, and my career in particular.

Ceri was strict and didn't take any nonsense from children, but he was a great fellow deep down. I was fortunate enough during that first term to get selected to play wing-forward for the school's under-14s team. A few practice sessions coincided with biology lessons. 'No, you can't go,' would be his first response every time, but a few minutes later he'd say, 'Off you go, and don't come back here with a broken leg.' I didn't enjoy PE lessons very much, and I can still vividly remember the smell of the gym – a combination of sweat and wax – as well as the rows of black canvas shoes that we had to wear. I lacked confidence in the gym, but out on the field I knew that I had something to offer and wasn't frightened of anyone or anything. This soon became apparent to Alwyn Nolan, and he was very supportive of the boy from Mynyddygarreg who was prepared to tackle each and every opponent, whatever their size.

At the end of term, I remember Dad talking about his aspirations for me, and making no bones about it. He wanted me to be an outside-half like Cliff Morgan, as well as a hundred-yard sprinter in athletics. I didn't manage to become either of those things! I nearly always played centre in rugby, and was a hurdler in school. He tried his best to turn me into a sprinter; when both of us were out hunting on the mountain, there'd be a sudden cry of 'down tools' – gun down, the ferret in its sack, nets secured and Mac commanded to look after everything – and Dad would challenge me to an eighty-yard race. At the beginning, he won every time, but year on year, I became faster, until I could beat him – which made him beam with delight. He was a strong, fit man who regularly walked for miles and miles, and still played rugby every Saturday.

But during that summer, before I started Secondary School, everything changed. By now, Dad was a repairer, which meant that he worked underground, fixing equipment and such like. One day, he was called to a tunnel where there had been heavy subsidence.

Dad – my great childhood hero.

Realising that he had to move an extremely heavy piece of metal, he tried to lift the weight without a second thought. A sharp, excruciating pain shot through his back. He couldn't move an arm or leg – he was totally paralysed for an instant.

As it was the school holiday, I happened to be at home that day. Towards the end of the afternoon, I remember seeing him coming towards the house. He was literally on all fours: he'd get up and move a few steps before falling down again on to his hands and knees. I went out to meet him and realised that he was in agony. We called the doctor and Dad was prescribed a course of De Witts tablets (whatever they were) to try to ease the pain in his back. After a month or five weeks, the pain began to relent, and Dad went back to work. But after a few weeks, the pain returned and a medical examination revealed that he'd injured several discs in his back. Before long, he had to start wearing a corset to keep his back straight, and a long period of chronic agonizing pain began. The radio became a great comfort to him, and he loved listening to all kinds of sports, especially boxing. He bought me two pairs of boxing gloves, and Peter Leyton and I spent endless hours pretending to be world champions, and even today, my knowledge of Rocky Marciano's career is far greater than my understanding of academic subjects!

One thing that I've never managed to overcome, to this day, is my fear of the dark – even though Dad tried his best to help me. When we came back late in the afternoon, just as it was about to get dark, Dad would insist on walking home without me: he'd walk one path, and I'd take another. By now, I was responsible for carrying the gun and I've often felt grateful that no one ever confronted me as I was creeping past Glanhiraeth; I probably would have used the gun, out of fear. The dark, just like the first day at school, was unknown territory and it filled me with dread. Despite this, school exams didn't cause a lot of stress or worry for me at that time, and I did well enough to ensure that I could sit the Thirteen Plus the following year. Mam and Dad were extremely pleased about this, so I put in an even bigger effort. Occasionally, when I misbehaved, Dad punished me quite severely, and my ears rang for hours after having a good clout from him. But there's one thing that I can say in all honesty – I never once lied to him, partly because the punishment for lying would be worse than anything else, but mainly because I had great respect for him.

During the following year, my aim, above all else, was passing the Thirteen Plus. Having the opportunity to go to Carmarthen Gram was my ambition – perhaps my greatest ambition ever, apart from playing for Wales. The morning of the results is still fresh in my mind. During assembly at school, Mr Williams, the deputy head, announced that two or three had been successful – and that Raymond Gravell was one of those. I waited impatiently for the bell to ring at the end of a very long day, and had to listen to countless words of advice from the Burry Port teachers about all the hard work and effort that was expected of me. But at last, I got home, and pretended to Dad that I hadn't passed – but the smile on my face betrayed me, revealing my glowing pride. And Dad beamed too, when he realised that I was going to the Gram. It was my first taste of success, and the joy it gave my parents made it even sweeter. My father and I had a very close relationship, and I remember spending hours with him, doing nothing apart from chatting. During that time, when I looked after the ferret, the goats and the rabbits, Dad taught me about sex, in full, and also cautioned me to behave properly with girls.

School matches were played on Wednesday afternoons, so the weekends were usually free for me to spend some time with Dad, wandering the mountain and hunting. By now, he walked much more slowly and had to stop every fifty yards or so to lean on a stone wall or a tree trunk to alleviate his pain. Unfortunately, his condition was deteriorating. He was put in a plaster cast, from the neck down to his hips. Every movement caused him pain, and every pain was excruciating. He spent days in bed on his back, in constant agony, until suddenly, in a bout of frustration, he'd get up to relieve the pain. That summer, I took his place at the local farms to help with the hay harvest. Now and again, the pain would ease enough for him to come with me for a little walk to the mountain, with Mac hot on our heels, but after a few steps, he'd say 'You go on', and would then give me detailed instructions for finding rabbits. He wore the plaster for nearly six months, and the distress that it caused was as severe as the physical pain. Even simple things – such as using the toilet – were stressful. I had to help him wash and keep clean. In a way, perhaps it brought us closer together, but I'm certain that handing over his responsibilities to Mam and me – carrying sacks of coal, for example, and looking after the animals – added to his mental torment. Even though I now realised that something graver than back pain was troubling him, I didn't realise the severity of his condition until he asked me to get Albert James, Mam-gu's brother, to help him with the garden. Albert used to cut my hair free of charge, but Dad would hand me a packet of Woodbines to give him now and again. Fair play to him, Albert came, and Dad leaned against the wall and began ordering us around. Albert sang old favourites as he worked, such as '*Arafa Don*' and '*Hen ŵr eisteddai wrth y tân*'; he had a rich, smooth voice and sang with real gusto.

Within a few months, I had to tell Dad that Albert had died. Once again, Dad was confined to his bed and this was the first time that I saw him crying – tears were streaming down his face, and I was a boy of thirteen with no idea how to react or what to do. He broke down completely. This was the end of the world for him – not only was he unable to work in the garden that summer, his assistant had left him too. Apart from Mam, the garden was his most treasured possession. It was never 'Come to see our new furniture' or 'new car' – it was 'Come to see the kidney beans.' That was one of the most popular topics of conversation amongst miners – comparing vegetables and the success or failure of various crops.

After a few weeks, I donned my little navy coat, emblazoned with the Gram's badge and the proverb '*Nid da lle gellir gwell*', ('Nothing is good where better is possible') and travelled to a different direction to begin a new school. That morning, the Eynon's bus stopped outside the iron gates of the Gram, and the

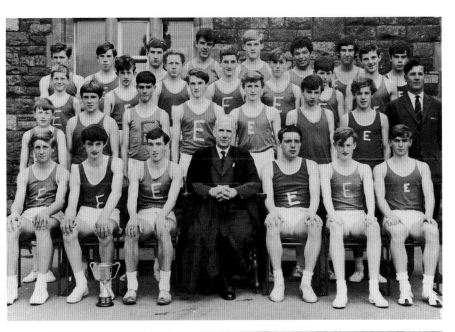

The Gram's Athletics team in Carmarthen 1966. Roy Bergiers is far left in the front row, whilst I'm just behind the headmaster, Bryn Howell (on the left).

Captaining Carmarthen Gram's Under-15 team, 1966-67.

road through the gate winding up to the old, prestigious school. I went to class 4W – W indicating the Welsh-language stream – and as in Burry Port school, I followed a row of boys to morning assembly. There, the headmaster, Bryn Howell, stood in his long black gown. I'd heard a lot about Bryn Howell from other boys from the village who went to the Gram – but now that legendary figure was standing on stage in front of me. I also met my class teacher for the first time, Glyndwr Walker, who did everything he could to help me settle in. I was aware of the school's rugby tradition as well, and before long, I came face to face with Elwyn Roberts, the PE teacher.

Elwyn had clear-cut ideas about rugby, not only as a sport but also as an activity that helped to develop a child's personality and character. To Elwyn Roberts, playing an open game with skill and flair was more important than winning. We didn't always see eye to eye but, as time passed, the two of us became closer. I got it into my head that Elwyn was English through and through, but after a while, I realized that he was a miner's son from Ebbw Vale, and I'm sure that this realisation brought us closer together. He decided that I had a talent for rugby, and so I was sent to play scrum-half in the trial for the Carmarthen and District team in the Dewar Shield Competition. Brynmor Roberts and Glyn Davies were in charge of the team, two men who had a great influence on me that season.

The changing room at Carmarthen Park was underneath the stand, and the sound of the studs still echoes in my ears now, as I think of us running onto the field in our green shirts to start playing against Mynydd Mawr schools, if I remember correctly. About ten minutes from kick-off, I saw none other but Dad, leaning against the steel railing which surrounded the field. For some reason that I can't really explain, I felt very resentful towards him for coming to watch me play. Perhaps I should have realized that the match meant a lot to him, but there we are, I was a headstrong teenager and I felt embarrassed in front of the other boys because my father had come along to watch me playing. At the end of the game, I regret to say that I expressed my annoyance, loud and clear, and told him that I never wanted him to watch me play again. 'Right, I'll never come again,' he said . . . and he never did. My reaction was a bit of a shock for him . . . and also a disappointment. We'd often argue with each other at home, but those occasions were completely private. The match, I suppose, was a public performance for me, and having my father there watching me made me feel somewhat less important. Dad was always true to his word. If 'No' was his response, 'No' would be the final word – there would be no turning back later. If he promised to meet me at five o'clock, he would be there on the dot. So, I knew that 'I'll never come again' meant exactly that.

But despite the disagreement at Carmarthen Park that Saturday, he still gave me a lengthy interrogation whenever I came home from a match. He was keen to know how the match had gone, what kind of game did I have, did I make every tackle, and what about my passing skills? That last question was a bit of a joke for us both, because even though I was a scrum-half, the quality of my service was atrocious at that time. Roy Bergiers was the outside-half, and he must have been blessed with very good hands, considering how poor some of my passes were. After every home game, we'd go for a meal at Morgan's restaurant on Lammas Street in Carmarthen. The 'restaurant' was really a fish and chip shop, but Glyn Davies and Brynmor Roberts would lead us there from the Park, past the Milford pub, and we'd sit down for a proper meal with a knife and fork – which made us feel very important! The first half of that season went remarkably well for this fourteen-year-old boy, and around Christmas time I was chosen to play in the first trial for the Welsh Schools team, to be held the following January.

I was on top of the world, and Dad was thrilled for me. But not everything was going well. Dad's back was getting worse, and looking back, I can see that everything was weighing heavily on his mind. I'm convinced now that Dad had already decided to end everything before that Christmas. To all intents and purposes, his hunting days were over, and he'd only take his gun out of the house occasionally. The dog was his only companion when he went for a walk to the mountain. I never heard my parents arguing, certainly never in front of me, and although I vaguely remember voices being raised a few times after I'd gone to bed, they never disagreed in front of me. Both stuck to the simple rule of never going to sleep feeling resentful towards each other. I never called Mam '*ti*' (informal 'you'): she was always '*chi*', and that was because Dad always preached: 'You only get one mother; respect her.' I never thought that was important at the time, and I always used '*ti*' when I spoke to Dad. My parents loved each other very much. But by now, Dad felt that he'd lost his self-respect because everything was beyond his ability. He was almost helpless. His only joy in life was asking me about the match when I came home every Saturday.

Much later in life, I realized that one of his main problems was his inability to talk about his problems and fears. I'm certain that he went through hell during those months, due to the physical pain and mental turmoil, without confiding in anyone. He'd bought Brynhyfryd for three hundred pounds, hoping to renovate the cottage and install a proper bathroom, as he'd promised Mam when they left Heol Gwelfor. But as he could no longer work, and without much money coming in, it was impossible for him to fulfil his promises. Before his accident, he worked double shifts for days, whenever he could, to save money to buy and renovate Brynhyfryd, but now his dreams had been shattered.

On the second Saturday of January, I was playing in the trial at Ammanford. It was a cold afternoon and the field was covered in mud. I got to play for two thirds of the trial: one third for the Whites and another for the Reds. I wasn't outstanding, but I didn't mess things up either, though I remember someone tearing my shirt to shreds in one maul. At the end of the trial, they announced the names of the players who would represent West Wales in the next trial, and I was selected as a reserve for the Reds. I arrived home just before it got dark, ready to face Dad and his barrage of questions about the day, but strangely, he wasn't there. Mam explained that he decided to go out with his gun mid-afternoon. I was surprised to hear this, as I'd been responsible for carrying the gun for some time now, but perhaps he was feeling better than usual and fancied a bit of hunting on the mountain. I didn't think much more of it, and neither did Mam. He'd taken Mac with him, so I sat down to talk to Mam about the trial and waited for Dad to come home. After it got dark, both of us felt very tense. It was eight o'clock. By now, I was walking round the back of the house every few minutes or so, in case I saw some sign of him. But I could see nothing, apart from the dark shadows of the mountain.

By half past nine, I knew that something was terribly wrong. Poor Mam was beside herself with worry, and kept walking back and forth from one room to another, from door to door, still trying to hide her anxiety from me. In the end, I decided that we had to look for him. I went to see Dai Evans and John Dennis to ask for their company and their help, because Mam wouldn't let me go to the mountain on my own and, to be completely honest, the idea of going by myself into the darkness was terrifying. By now, I was convinced that an accident had happened, and so began the worst journey I've ever had to face. Dai and John followed us with lamps, but from the moment I reached the mountain, I never once turned around. I didn't think for a second about where I was going; it was as if something was pulling me every step of the way. It didn't cross my mind that I should look here or there or at another part of the path, nor that I should turn my lamp towards some shrubs or hedges. Rhydian, the blacksmith's son, had a barn on the mountain side, but I walked straight past it until I came to the place where my father lay, in a shallow ditch in the ground, on the mountain top. I'd been shouting 'Dadi' and 'Mac' since leaving the house, and as I approached the mountain top, I could hear Mac running towards me through the bracken. He ran up, and tried to lick me, before pulling me towards Dad's resting place.

I rushed forward, but as I touched his clothes I knew that it was all over. That second, I remember, was one of the longest I'd ever experienced – the split second between discovering Dad's body and completely breaking down. I was led back to the village to Audrey and Dai's house, and John and Dai went to break the news to Mam. I've been told that lifting the body was very difficult, with old Mac fiercely defending his master. Ifan Gravell, Dad's cousin, had to get some men from the village to pull Mac off my father. He was faithful to Dad till the end. I wasn't up to the job of telling Mam: I was too cowardly to do it, and it still pains me that I failed to carry out my duty. That night, Mam and I stayed the night with John and Eirwen, who were close family friends. The doctor insisted that we took some sleeping tablets, and my last memory of that night is lying in bed by Mam's side, begging her to close her eyes and try to sleep. I could be wrong, but I have a feeling that she didn't sleep a wink that night, not even with the doctor's tablets. I can see her eyes now – her unblinking gaze fixed on a spot on the ceiling. She didn't say a word. Dad's death was the end of the world for her and I was completely broken too. How could I look after Mam; how could I face tomorrow without Dad? For days afterwards, dozens of people came to see us and I had to explain to them – as well as the inquest – what happened that awful night when Dad shot himself dead with his double-barrel gun.

Two incidents in the days following Dad's death made me reconsider everything. The first occurred when the body came back to the house, and I insisted on seeing Dad and touching his face. I knew, instantly, that Dad wasn't the person in the coffin, and that it was a kind of shell – but not my father. The second incident happened on the day of the funeral. Poor Mam couldn't cope with it. Hundreds of people came to grieve with her and to pay their last respects to a very popular man amongst his friends and colleagues. We were both very grateful to the Reverend Gwyn Davies Jones, the preacher, for presiding over the service with such skilful assurance. After being taken to the cemetery and the graveside, I couldn't hold it in any longer and burst into tears. Realizing that I'd lost a special and unique person in my life, I became inconsolable: he was an adviser, friend, brother and father. I cried those bitter tears for many years.

Mynyddygarreg – the Mountain of Stone.

Evading a tackle at Stradey during the early 1970s, against the Harlequins. Who'd have thought that I would actually represent this most English of teams in France in 1974!

4

Loss

The weeks following the tragedy were a period of existing rather than living. Discovering Dad's body was a nightmare that haunted me every time I closed my eyes, and if it were up to me, I wouldn't have faced people at all. But I was persuaded by Glyn Davies and Brynmor Roberts to travel to London to play for Carmarthenshire's under-15s team against London Counties at Esher. I stayed with one of my opponents, a little scrum-half called Mark Wynter – who went on to play scrum-half for the English Schoolboys team. And believe it or not, one of our centres in that game was Meredydd James, who rose to prominence later as a member of Bridgend's front row as well as their captain. Despite the fun and camaraderie around me on the bus journey to London, I'd slip into my own little world from time to time. On the way back, one of the boys had a cassette player, and was playing the Simon and Garfunkel song 'Homeward Bound'; memories and emotions came flooding back as I returned to my family and neighbours.

The following Monday, I really wasn't ready to face people, but I reluctantly went back to the Gram. There was one teacher in particular, however, who helped me overcome my grief, and my gratitude to Glyndwr Walker for his friendship and advice during that period is more than I could ever say. He went out of his way to look for me to say a few words of sympathy, which raised my spirits immensely. On top of that, playing every Saturday morning for the local team helped to ease the pain. But returning home at the end of the afternoon was still a distressing experience, as there was an unnatural silence weighing down on Brynhyfryd. Over the years, grabbing the gun and going hunting had become a habit; I'd then clean and dismantle the gun, and enjoy the whole process of handling it. But this came to an end. Mam decided that she never wanted me near the gun again. To Mam, the gun embodied something that took away her beloved husband, and by now I can understand her pain and distress. But to me, the gun had only a marginal connection with the tragedy. After all, Dad had taken the decision to end his pain and suffering, and strangely enough I still believe that the gun, in a way, was his friend. Without the gun, he would have found another way to end his life.

I love being in the company of others, but I also love daydreaming, and being on my own with nature. The silence and solitude gives me peace of mind, and shuts out the world and its problems for a while. From those days onwards, Mam became much more protective of me, and if I came back late from somewhere, her face would be a picture of anxiety. I soon realized that I always had to be true to my word with Mam, and if I said that I'd be home at a certain time, I'd have to stick to it. Years later, I found out many things about Mam that I never knew before. She lost her father at a young age (he drowned in the Gwendraeth estuary), her brother died after a long, painful illness, and then her husband. Each loss left her wounded, and as a consequence she became a stronger and tougher character. After a few months, she realized that she couldn't support me on her widow's pension and decided that she had to earn a living for us both. She got a job at the optical factory in Kidwelly, and as she became accustomed to leaving the house every day, her *hiraeth* was alleviated to some extent.

In school, I was facing my first exams, and had got to a point where I'd lost all interest in schoolwork. The only thing I remember enjoying during that period was reading *Cysgod y Cryman* and *Yn ôl i Leifior* by Islwyn Ffowc Elis, for my Welsh O Level, and perhaps that enjoyment stemmed from my interest in nature and the countryside. I didn't derive any pleasure from studying anything else, and that became apparent when I had my annual school report! That summer, like many other boys, I started looking for a holiday job, and got some labouring work with MLM in Kidwelly.

Digging gutters and tunnels for water pipes and sewerage was hard work, but I relished the opportunity to get to know some of Carmarthenshire's loveliest places, such as Meidrim and Tre-lech, and a particularly wonderful place in the same area, Gelli-wen. The most important thing that summer was 'doing my bit' to bring some money home. Mam's job involved working all day with a red powdery substance, used to make lenses for glasses – 'rouge' was the term for it – and I can still see her coming back from work with her red-stained apron. Eventually, that job had a detrimental effect on her hands, which meant that she had to give it up within two years. Her arthritis worsened and regular treatments at Glangwili hospital in Carmarthen became necessary.

My weeks with MLM that summer were pure pleasure. I started to grow up, through working with men that were much older than I was, many of whom had been my father's friends. Fair play, they looked after me extremely well. However, September came much too soon, and I had to take off my work clothes and replace them with my black blazer and school tie, ready for the O Levels in class 5W. But rugby was my main interest. Elwyn Roberts, the PE teacher, decided that the boys would no longer be allowed to play for the district team; the school would have its own team instead. Although he realized that I wouldn't be able to win a cap for the Wales Schoolboys team, he persuaded me soon enough that playing for the school was the most important thing, and I was appointed team captain. Also, I got the chance to play a few games during the season for the school's first team, and playing with eighteen and nineteen-year-old boys was a big challenge for me. The game against Lampeter School that season has stuck in my mind. I went down on the ball at the exact second that one of the Lampeter players decided to kick the ball all the way to Aberaeron. I'm afraid that my teeth, rather than the ball, shot to Aberaeron that morning! I spent the weekend in considerable pain, and the following Monday morning, Bertram Rees, the dentist, took out four tooth stumps. For weeks afterwards, I was very conscious of the fact that I looked like Dracula – a very depressing feeling for a fifteen-year-old boy trying to impress the girls!

Amongst this hurly-burly, I was occasionally reminded of the imminent O Level examinations, but I'm ashamed to say that I didn't put a lot of effort into the seven subjects I took – and I regret it to this day. Mam wanted me to be happy and tried to ensure that I wouldn't 'go off the rails', so she never pushed me with my schoolwork. Perhaps things would have been different if Dad had been alive.

I remember playing in a seven-a-side match in Ferryside one evening before an exam, where my knee was badly bumped. It became swollen like a pumpkin and I went to the exam the next day with a walking stick. Bryn Howell, the headmaster, couldn't understand why I needed the stick, but I managed not to disclose anything about the previous night's events. I can't say that my results shook the foundations of academia, though I did pass the Welsh exam. But at the time, it was far more important for me to earn a wage, and spend another summer working for MLM.

In August, I decided that I wanted to go back to school, and I joined a new class that had been formed for those who'd failed their examinations. 5 X – like those film classifications – caused a bit of an X to the teachers that year. The new CSE had been established, and I was one of its guinea pigs, along with Charlie Thomas who went on to play with me at Stradey. (Charlie is Imogen's father, the beautiful girl who became a star on *Big Brother*). I realised that I was too young to take on any kind of apprenticeship, but having the opportunity to play for the school's first team was perhaps my main reason for returning. Just a week into the new term, I was playing scrum-half for the first team, whose captain that season was the winger D. A. Morgan. The outside-half was Roy Bergiers, who became my fellow centre at Stradey and for Wales, and we had another successful season. The highlight for me was travelling to Oxford mid-week to play against Oriel College. It was a memorable visit as we played against a team of men, and were naturally treated like men by our opponents. Without doubt, I was the baby of the team, and I'll always remember a pub called The Bear, where I had a few pints with fellow players who were much older than I was. I ended up losing my false teeth somewhere in Oxford that night.

Growing up could be a painful process sometimes. During that season, as the only member of 5X in the school's first team, I came to realize that rugby was a game that required a lot of thinking and analysing – and Elwyn Roberts certainly thought very deeply about it. When the time came for us to play

Me, Roy Bergiers, Gareth Roberts and Richard Moriarty bust a gut to catch Bill Osborne in the game between West Wales and New Zealand in 1978.

against Llanelli Grammar School – the big match for both schools – I was put in as the number eight, because Elwyn had decided that it would be the best way of preventing Llanelli's centre from winning the game. That centre was Keith Hughes, who would go on to play for London Welsh and Wales in a few years time. My tackling had always been one of my strengths, and by running across the field – just like Alun Pask for Wales – I brought him down with a strong tackle, which kept him quiet for the rest of the game. And our team won.

Phil weaving his magic at Stradey against Northampton. Nigel Howells outside him and Alun Davies, Roger Powell, Derek and JJ screaming, 'Go on your own, Phil.'

At the end of the season, I was selected as the school team's centre for the first time, and also had a cap for Carmarthenshire Schools against London Counties. To top it all, I was advised by Elwyn Robets to go to Stradey Park to train with Llanelli's seven-a-side team, which is where I met Phil Bennett for the first time. This was my first encounter with the Llanelli club, and I spent those evenings at Stradey playing against the seven players selected to represent Llanelli. More tackle practice for me! Back in school, I decided at last that I needed some sort of qualifications, and with a little more effort, I managed to pass six CSEs. But once again, I had to make a decision about my future. Would it be worthwhile for me to return to school, at nearly seventeen years old? I delayed that decision for about two months by knocking on the door of the washeries at Coedbach, between Kidwelly and Trimsaran, where I asked for some temporary coal-washing work. Those two months helped me reach a decision, as I enjoyed being in the company of adults and had a warm welcome from people like Jacko Hurley and Hughie Walters who were close friends of my father's before he died. My job meant getting there early, lighting the fire and cleaning the canteen so that it was ready for the workers; then down to the 'wash' to help out, as and when needed. There weren't any showers there, so I'd have to walk two miles to get home, covered from head to toe in coal dust, and have a bath in front of the fire, exactly as Dad used to do.

It was during those months that I developed a stronger awareness of my Welsh heritage. It was the year of the investiture, and Dafydd Iwan's songs ignited an awakening in me. I watched him on the television programme *Y Dydd*, but '*Carlo*' and '*Croeso 69*' were the songs that really made me realize that we are a separate nation, and that our language and culture and way of life are totally different from those of other nations. My simple enjoyment of the songs was the first spark, but the awareness developed into something much more profound. On a Saturday night, however, I'd follow many of my friends to the dance, either in St Peter's Hall or the Barracks in Carmarthen. I met a girl from Meidrim there, who worked for the Health Board. Her name was Aurona Rees, and I plucked up the courage to ask her for a dance. At the end of the evening, she caught the last bus to Meidrim at ten o'clock, and I caught the last bus at ten to ten to Mynyddygarreg!

The seven-a-side competition in the Gwendraeth Valley that summer was held to celebrate the investiture – or that was the excuse, anyway – and we formed a team in Mynyddygarreg. Luckily, we won the Felinfoel Challenge Cup, which was the youth competition. Who was sat there, watching the final round, but Peter Rees, chairman of Llanelli Rugby Club. He came up to me and asked me to play for the Llanelli youth team, if I didn't want to go back to school. I decided there and then that there was no way I was going back to school! I had to search for work, and after looking around and making a few enquiries, I was offered a job by David Sayers, a friend of the late Bert Peel, with the South Wales Electricity Board, as a measurer for Llanelli's shops and public buildings. I became an expert in holding one end of a tape measure and jotting down figures on hundreds of pages. On the rugby field, after many trial matches for the youth team, I was selected as a centre for the team, and had a remarkably successful season with them.

Before Christmas, I had two reasons to celebrate: I got a permanent job with the Electricity Board and was selected for the West Wales team, with Gareth Jenkins as captain, in the first trial for the Wales youth team at Aberavon. It must have gone quite well, as I was selected for the final trial at Caerphilly. There never was a worse day for a rugby match; it rained heavily for days on end, and on the afternoon of the match, the rain hammered down even more heavily. But luckily again, I impressed the selectors and the coach Ieuan Evans. I was selected to represent the Wales youth team at St Helen's in Swansea against the Wales schools team. I was fortunate that Glanmor, Aurona's elder brother, agreed to drive me around on many occasions that season, and his kindness was exceptional as he'd also take me all the way back to Aurona's home in Meidrim after a match! On the evening of the match against Wales Schools, everyone in the village wished me well, and a large contingent travelled down to support me in Swansea. There, under the floodlights, I scored the evening's winning try – and it was great to read about it in the paper the next day. The next match was against the English Colts at Abertillery, and then, in the last match of the season, I got my first cap against France at Figeac. That was quite an experience for me; travelling to a foreign country and having the first experience of flying to Paris, then catching an overnight train to the South of France. After arriving at Figeac on the Saturday, ready for the Sunday match, Bryn the Chemist from Pontyates, who was on the youth team committee, took me to my room at the hotel to show me the cap that I was about to win. At last, I was about to have a real international match, and wearing that red cap for the first time was quite a thrill.

These days we think of him as a coach, but let's be honest – Gareth Jenkins was one hell of a player.

When both teams stood in two rows before the first kick, in front of the comparatively small stand on the pitch, I felt a huge disappointment as the band played not '*Hen Wlad fy Nhadau*', but rather 'God Save the Queen'! My heart sank and my body filled with rage. I was furious, I must admit, and I'm sure that I tackled the French centres with more force than usual, with the fire of Welsh patriotism burning in my heart. Playing against the French is hard and difficult at all levels, so a 6-6 draw was a very satisfactory result.

The referee for that match was Larry Lamb, one of England's best referees, but that meant nothing to me at the time. That evening, having knocked back a few too many glasses of fine French wine, I turned to a handsome, smartly dressed man by the bar at the hotel, and speaking in English with a French accent (hoping that every Frenchman present would get the joke!) I asked him to explain the motifs on his elegant tie. He answered, in the Queen's best English, that it was the English Referees' Association tie, and that he had been refereeing the match that afternoon. He looked at me quite suspiciously when I said that I hadn't recognised him in his clothes! He's reminded me of this story many times since.

Ieuan Evans, Llanelli's first coach.

Back at Stradey Park, if I remember correctly, we won every tournament that year. At the end of the international season, many of us had the chance to train with the first team and their coach, the legendary Carwyn James. Listening to Carwyn and obeying his orders was a valuable experience for a young man. In April 1970, I was given my first chance to play for Llanelli's first team against Lampeter Rugby Club – the place where, a few years earlier, I'd lost four teeth! Llanelli were invited to Lampeter to celebrate the inauguration of their new floodlights. As it was a mid-week game, many experienced players couldn't be there so I had the opportunity to wear the Scarlet shirt for the first time. After the match, we had a few pints in Lampeter before heading back, and by then it was raining heavily. By the time we reached Kidwelly, it was the early hours of the morning, and I was too shy to tell Peter Rees, the chairman, that I had to walk two and a half miles through the pouring rain to get home. I was soaked through by the time I reached Mynyddygarreg around three o'clock in the morning. But despite the weather, I felt happy knowing that my rugby career was on the way up.

5

Stradey Park

During the summer of 1970, I was reminded that the club would begin training again towards the end of July; and so, I polished my boots with more elbow grease than usual, just in case; after all, little things make all the difference sometimes. After the first training session, on a warm July evening, I went into the clubhouse for a pint after a shower, where I had the chance to talk to the Chairman, Peter Rees. I told him that I was going to play in the trials for Kidwelly within a few weeks, as I didn't think that I had any chance of playing for Llanelli. He disagreed, and felt certain that I'd have plenty of opportunities to wear the scarlet shirt at Stradey Park. The following week, Clive John (Barry's brother) came up to me during a training session to tell me the same thing, and of course, hearing this from the captain gave me a bit of a boost and made me think that perhaps I could have a few games after all.

The home of Llanelli RFC since the 1880s – Stradey Park. It's hard to belive that the club is bidding it farewell.

At the time, in August 1970, I didn't dream that I'd represent Llanelli thirty times during that season. Traditionally, Llanelli's first official match was against Pontypridd at Stradey Park. I was over the moon when I saw my name on the list at centre. My golden opportunity was here: it wasn't an end-of-season match, but rather a first-class match, in front of the Stradey crowd, with the boy from Mynyddygarreg playing against experienced players such as Joe Smith, Colin Riley and Ritchie Hope. Even in those days, I wasn't a big fitness fanatic, but every evening I'd force myself to run three or four miles around the mountain, before undoing my good work with a pint at the Greenfield pub in the village. On the Friday night before the match, I remember going there as usual, and all the regulars wishing me well for the next day and refusing to let me drink that evening! Apart from representing Wales, nothing could beat the thrill of running out onto Stradey Park in front of a huge crowd. I had a good game against Pontypridd, and rugby commentators were complimentary about my hard tackling as well as the way I created a try for winger Andy Hill on the Pwll side of the pitch. But I was aware that my passing was poor then – as a few irate wingers pointed out to me that season – but no one could criticize my total commitment when it came to the tackle. It's possible that playing against much older boys on Cae'r Post had toughened me up, as my strength in the tackle had also impressed my schoolteachers.

Carwyn James was the coach at Stradey Park that season, and he persuaded Tom Hudson to assist him. I became very fond of Tom, if only for one thing: he'd never ask players to do anything that he couldn't do himself. At the time, he was a lecturer at Swansea University, and he was very fortunate that he had very exciting and talented individuals such as John Thomas, Gwyn Ashby and Allan Lewis (a student at Loughborough College at the time) to coach at Stradey.

If I had to choose the most talented player of the early 1970s, I'd put Allan Lewis head and shoulders above everyone else. At the time, he showed great promise that would have taken him, without doubt, to the Wales team and the Lions. But just before Christmas 1970, we were playing against Swansea at Stradey Park – with Allan Lewis and me at centre, Phil Bennett at outside-half, and Roy Mathias on the wing. During the match, Allan was tackled awkwardly – I'll never forget the crack and his piercing scream. The match stopped instantly – the referee didn't even have to blow his whistle; Allan's leg had been shattered, and the only thing I could hear was the sound of a rabbit screeching in pain after I'd shot it without killing it. Allan's injury – and seeing him being carried off the pitch on a stretcher, still screaming in agony – was a horrific experience. I was frozen on the spot, and Phil Bennett had to drag me away. That match stayed in my mind, as five players had to leave the field. Despite this, no one would have called it a dirty game. It was certainly a tough game, and I think that the game at the beginning of the 1970s was much tougher than it is today. There were a few idiots around, as there are today, but referees in those days could differentiate between dirty and hard play. Unfortunately, Wales lost the services of one of its most talented centres that afternoon, and he was so badly injured that he never got back to full fitness.

Had it not been for an injury, Allan Lewis would have played for Wales and the Lions. A dear friend.

During those first few months with Llanelli, I realised that I was a boy playing a man's game. Everything on the pitch happened much more quickly, and the game was certainly much more physical than in youth team matches. On top of this, the Stradey crowd expected much more of their players; after all, the relationship between the supporters and the players at Stradey is unique – it's as if the supporters own the players, and demand the highest possible standard of each one of them on the field. The main reason I was accepted by the Stradey crowd was my tackling. A strong tackle would almost inspire as much fervour in the crowd as a beautiful try. I also became aware, when I read match reports, of the press's power and influence. Almost immediately, a few reporters, such as Bleddyn Williams, were saying that I should have a trial for Wales, but I knew very well that I was far from ready to move onto the next level. I had a very long way to go, if people only looked at the way I passed the ball! But Stradey supporters, especially the older generation, venerated heroic hard tacklers such as Albert Jenkins, and later Cyril Davies and Terry Davies, which was a big boost for me, especially when I was mentioned in the same breath as them.

I was thrilled to be playing for Llanelli that season, but being selected to play for Carmarthenshire was an extra bonus. I must admit that playing for the county gave me much more personal satisfaction than it did some of the other players. After all, the Welsh counties' Western Mail cup was not as highly regarded as the English counties' tournament. But for me, representing my own patch was very important. I was chosen to play against Breconshire at Brynamman. John Thomas and I had to ask for Carwyn's permission to play. He let us go, provided that we came straight back for training at Stradey after playing that afternoon at Brynamman. And since it was Carwyn who'd said so, we didn't have a choice; thinking about it now, I wouldn't have dared to disobey him, being the baby of the team at the time. Having said that, wearing the county's shirt was an important step forward, and I thoroughly enjoyed playing those games throughout my career. Playing for the county gave me my first opportunity to travel to North Wales, and I fell head over heels in love with the area north of Machynlleth. But that's another story.

One of the highlights of that first season was playing at the Arms Park for the first time against Cardiff. It had always been an important match, which was regarded by many as a battle between east and west. It seemed that the battle was about to get bloodier. In Llanelli's back row, two brothers were playing, Clive and Alan John, while the third brother, Barry, was Cardiff's outside-half. In the week before the match, the press had a field day discussing the 'family feud' that would be played out on the field. The atmosphere at the beginning of the match was electric. At the first lineout, there was a fierce clash between Alan John and John Hickey, a member of Cardiff's back row. Watching the brawl, I realised once again that I was playing a man's game. I soon learned another lesson, when Phil Bennett launched a towering kick into the Cardiff 22. Barry John stood underneath, his steady hands poised to take the ball. I ran towards him as quickly as I could, but by the time I tackled him, Barry had punted the ball over our heads towards the line. It was a late tackle, and naturally, I apologized to Barry, but Phil Bennett gave me a mouthful – for not tackling him harder! Llanelli managed to cross the line three times that afternoon, but Clive and Alan spent the whole afternoon chasing their little brother's shadow around the Arms Park. At the end of that game, Barry was beaming, having dropped four goals and ensured victory for the Blue-and-blacks, 12-9.

During that early period, I was very fortunate to have employers who were very supportive of my desire to play rugby, and it was never a problem to have time off to represent the club or the county. Indeed, my photograph appeared more often in the Electricity Board magazine than the *Western Mail* and *Evening Post* put together. I'm sure that I gave them some good publicity, and that, of course, suited me too! At the end of the season, the club's blazer badge was presented to me during the annual dinner. At least thirty matches had to be played in order to merit this honour, and I wore the badge with pride from that moment onwards. During the final half of the '70/'71 season, there were strong rumours around Llanelli that Carwyn was likely to be chosen to lead the Lions to New Zealand in the summer of '71; voices were also heard at Stradey Park discussing the players most likely to join him.

Carwyn was indeed chosen as coach, and when the names of the squad were announced at the end of the international season, they included Delme Thomas and Derek Quinnell, two Llanelli players – even though Quinnell had never represented Wales. Barry Llewelyn was invited to go on the tour, but declined the invitation. The season was successful for me personally, and in addition to the blazer badge, I was part of the team that beat Ebbw Vale in the final of the Floodlight Alliance at Stradey.

By now, I – reluctantly – was responsible for the garden at home, but thankfully, Glanmor came up from Meidrim to give me a hand and we planted enough potatoes, at least, to keep us going all winter. I must admit that I never enjoyed gardening very much. My life was already quite full, what with courting Aurona and rugby, and I could always find plenty of excuses for neglecting my gardening duties. Barbara, Dad's sister, and her husband, were a great help to Mam and me during those years after Dad passed away, and I often relied very heavily on them.

The Lions had an unforgettable summer in 1971, which has since passed into rugby folklore, and I loved listening to the radio commentary from New Zealand, dreaming that one day I'd get the chance to tour with the Lions. The Lions' talented back division continuously created mayhem, but nothing gave me more pleasure than hearing about Derek Quinnell and Delme Thomas, as we were quite good friends by then. I've said many times that I've always looked up to Delme Thomas – in the best possible way, though I also look up to him quite literally, as he's way over six foot tall! Delme was chosen to play for the Lions in 1966 (before he played for Wales) and was a pupil at Carmarthen Gram at the same time as I was. I remember seeing a photograph of him in the *Western Mail*. He was wearing a hard hat and climbing a telegraph pole – with arms of pure muscle – as part of his day job at the Electricity Board. For some reason or other, some electricians came to school once, one of whom was Colin Philips, Delme's brother-in-law. I, along with some other boys, started to wind him up by saying that Delme wasn't much of a player. He was furious. But the following Saturday, as I was waiting for Aurona outside Woolworth's in Carmarthen, I saw Colin, Delme and a few others walking towards me. Colin turned to me, and said, 'Now then, boy, tell Delme what you said to me about him.' I prayed – more than I've ever prayed in my life – for Carmarthen's pavement to swallow me whole. My face must have been as red as my hair. 'Oh! I was only joking Delme, honest now.' But the gentle giant laughed warmly, much to the relief of a deeply embarrassed young boy.

Delme was a prominent member of Llanelli's second row the next time I met him, and for some reason, we developed a very close friendship. I think it was partly due to our shared passion for Wales and all things Welsh, the fact that we both worked for the same company, and that I was courting a girl from Delme's area. He came from Bancyfelin, a few miles from Meidrim. But the main reason was that I always turned to him for advice – and fair play, I'm sure that I was often a bit of a nuisance, with my self-doubt and endless questioning. He was a very good adviser, and helped me deal with many tricky situations. His quiet reasoning was totally different from my hot-headed approach to things. Although Delme was often provoked and attacked by opponents, I never once saw him retaliate. He wasn't on the field to fight – he was there to leap and get the ball and win the lineouts. He was an extremely dignified man. I'd often get wound up about something or other, and then Delme's voice – quiet but firm – would appear from somewhere, saying 'Cool down, Gvav bach'. His voice, with its soft 'r', would always have a calming effect on me. He was a man of few words, but his strength and power shone through, giving strength and motivation to us youngsters in the team. Whenever the team had an away game, Delme would always sit in one of the front seats of the bus, and his first words would be 'Come and sit here, Gvav bach'. We would then put the world to rights, and talk about his favourite hobby – breeding birds.

Another chain was broken that summer, with the death of Mac, the dog. He was old, but I still took him out walking on the mountain, though those walks gradually became shorter as he couldn't walk very far. Dad had built him a kennel in the garden, with a long chain so that he could have a bit of a wander. But one day, when I went out to feed him, he had passed away. I felt that Mac had kept a part of my father's spirit alive, which had now disappeared. I was heartbroken – he was Dad's dog. But perhaps there was also a sense of relief, because I took the birds and traps to Dai Rhydodyn, an old friend of my father's, and sold the ferrets to local hunters. It was the end of an era. I spent my days digging holes for the Electricity Board, and though it was back-breaking

Welsh Cup Semi-final 1972. Back row: Derek Quinnell, Roy Thomas, Alan James, Hefin Jenkins, Tony Crocker, Roy Mathias, Delme Thomas.
Front row: Clive John, Roger Davies, me, Barry Llewelyn, Phil Bennett, Brian Fowler. Kneeling: Selwyn Williams and Andy Hill.

work, I found it quite enjoyable. Apart from strengthening my arms and body, there was plenty of fun and banter with the boys.

When the heroic Lions arrived back from New Zealand in August – heralded by cheers and praise as if they were gods – I, and the other mere mortals at Llanelli, were being coached by Tom Hudson once again. On the first night, we were led to believe that the fitness programme wouldn't be too hard, as we spent half an hour on the field, jogging and passing the ball to each other, finishing with some general exercises. Everyone turned up to the second training session in good spirits; after all, the first wasn't too bad. We were all chatting away whilst getting changed, when Tom walked in, all six foot three of him, a former paratrooper who came fourth in the Pentathlon at the Rome Olympics. His first words that evening were, 'Right, get ready to do some road running.' The circuit went from Stradey Park, along the main road to Burry Port, and down to Pembrey beach. This had to be completed without stopping, following a pattern of running half a mile, walking two hundred yards, and so on. When we got to the beach, there were more exercises, which involved running up and down sand dunes, before heading back to Stradey Park. Seeing those big red gates was a huge relief, and we were all looking forward to a shower and a good rest. But no, we had another hour of training on the field before finishing the session, and of course, there would be two sessions a week, on Monday and Wednesday, during August. The club had many successful years with Tom as coach, so the effectiveness of his fitness programme was never in any doubt.

The '71/72 season was again very successful in Llanelli's history, with further interest added following the Welsh Rugby Union's decision to hold the Welsh Cup for the first time in fifty-eight years. The Floodlight Alliance was won once again, and we got to the final round of the Cup at the beginning of May at the Arms Park against the All-blacks from Neath. The match was played on exactly the same day as the F.A. cup final at Wembley, which was a totally mad idea. Although a crowd of twelve thousand watched Neath giving us a good beating, I remember feeling that the Arms Park sounded and looked pretty empty that afternoon. It was quite disappointing to reach the final and play in front of a crowd no bigger than that of a good Saturday afternoon at Stradey. The result was an extra disappointment, though I must admit that Neath played far better than us on the day. I remember very clearly the sight of Dai Parker, Neath's diminutive outside-half, crossing for a wonderful try as if he'd run through the Llanelli full-back Roger Davies's legs! During that season, we played three times against Neath, and had beaten them every time, but the Welsh All-blacks reigned supreme and won the cup by fifteen points to nine.

The disappointment of losing to Neath in the Cup was eased to some extent by the fact that Llanelli had been invited to play six matches over three weeks that summer in the scorching heat of South Africa. To a young lad, the opportunity to travel to the other end of the world seemed like an enormous adventure. I'd like to take the opportunity here to express my gratitude to the Llanelli club, not only for the support and opportunities I was given, but also for the way that the club treated its players. During all those years that I was involved with the club, I never had to pay for any tour, whatever the distance travelled, from Tumble to Twickenham or Transvaal. I don't feel that I owe the club, or rugby itself, anything, but I have many things to be grateful for; in my own way, I hope that I made a valuable contribution to a game that I thoroughly enjoyed playing. This tour was one of the most pleasurable experiences, and although it provoked political demonstrations and fierce opposition from the press, I must admit that my attitude was completely selfish, and I was looking forward to the tour with great excitement.

The tour manager was Handel Greville, the club chairman, and the assistant-manager and coach was Norman Gale. Carwyn refused to travel to South Africa on moral grounds, and I'm sure that every player respected his beliefs, although they possibly disagreed with him. Politically, I was totally naïve at the time, and the political debates that went on didn't influence me either way – I wanted nothing more than to play rugby. A few weeks before the tour, I received a note from Ken Jones, the club secretary, asking me to go to Hodges clothes shop in Llanelli to get measured for trousers, a blazer and tie, and two shirts especially for the tour. It was the first time I'd ever been treated like this. A week later, on a training night, the shop staff came to Stradey to fit the clothes. They were ready a week later, and were worn in the official team photos.

My most vivid memory of the first match is the size of Eastern Province's front row; they were massive, and in the middle of the match I had to confront them when a brawl erupted between us. As I tried to stop the fight, a member of Eastern Province's front row planted his fist on my nose and broke it, although I wasn't aware of it at the time. Llanelli won that afternoon, and despite my painful nose I was pleased with the result as we travelled from Port Elizabeth to Utson to play against the Western Districts. It was there that I met an ostrich for the first time. There weren't many of those around Mynyddygarreg, so I jumped at the chance to ride one in South Africa. Chris Charles, the prop forward, didn't enjoy the experience as much as I did, as his ostrich decided to drop to the floor in protest under the strain of Chris's weight, and refused to budge an inch. Back on the rugby field, we triumphed there too, but then lost the third match of the tour against Boland – an extremely strong team – before moving onto Bloemfontein where we were up against the mighty Orange Free State. When we went out onto the field to play that game, I turned to Roy Bergiers and said, '*Duw*, look at the size of that forward.' His response was, 'He's not a forward, Grav, he's their centre!' I was face to face with Joggie Jansen, one of the strongest and most muscular centres I've ever seen. Needless to say, it was no surprise that we lost that match!

We then went on from Bloemfontein to the last game at Transvaal and, to all intents and purposes, this was a test match, and my fourth match on tour. We'd reached the point now where only fourteen of us were fully fit, and were just about to face a team that included Piet Greyling, one of the best wing-forwards ever to grace a rugby field, in my opinion. Because our casualties were so numerous, Gareth Jenkins had to play despite being injured, and in no time at all, a brawl developed between him and Piet Greyling. Like a fool, I decided to stick my oar in to help Gareth . . . well, to separate them at least. But Ziggy Sauermann, a member of the front row, appeared from somewhere and I didn't see his punch coming at all. I was struck on the side of my face, and I can only remember my legs quaking, like a boxer's legs, and feeling myself slowly sinking to the ground. It's the only time I've ever felt my legs turning to jelly underneath me. There I was, on my knees, trying to clear my head, and the next thing I remember is seeing Chris Charles literally flying through the air into Sauermann, and for a few minutes, rugby was the last thing on everyone's minds.

Llanelli lost that final match, and I have no recollection of the rest of the afternoon. I had the most agonizing headache of my life, and as we were so far above sea level, my nose started bleeding during the post-match dinner. Delme Thomas came to my rescue again that evening, and took me to my room and put me to bed, while everyone else was at our farewell party. I was aware of the noise in the background, and my estimation of Delme grew even more that evening as he'd been willing to sacrifice the party to look after me. Before sinking into a deep sleep that night, I was comforted by his words, 'Gvav, I'll kill anyone who dares come through this door tonight.' When I woke up the next morning, I felt like a new man and was ready to face the journey back to Wales. And a very memorable journey it was too, because of one special incident. As the plane was landing in Heathrow, Handel Greville announced that the players had to stay on the plane for a few minutes. I knew full well the reason for this, as rumours had been circulating for a while that a captain had to be selected for the club, for the '72/73 centenary season. During the long journey home, I had the chance to tell the hooker, Meirion Davies, that I wanted to nominate Delme as captain, and before I'd even finished, Meirion answered, 'I'll second you.' So, after the other travellers left the plane, the chairman called for the players' attention, and asked for our nominations.

Before he finished his sentence, I shouted out that I wanted to nominate Delme Thomas, and Meirion seconded the nomination straight away. I hadn't mentioned my intention to Delme, as I was certain that he'd oppose it with all his might. But in my eyes, he was our one and only choice at the time.

It was a unanimous decision. Delme was Llanelli's new captain. As we stepped down from the plane, Delme came over to me and said, 'What the hell have you done now, Gvav bach?' – and believe it or not, his voice was full of gratitude. As he put his arm on my shoulder, a wave of emotion came over me, and I felt extremely humble but also very proud that I'd nominated him. After all, his thoughtfulness and care for me on that tour was immeasurable, and for some reason I think that both of us had a feeling that something great was about to happen that season, in the club's centenary.

Celebrating Christmas on S4C's Heno, with friends Dafydd Iwan, Delme, Derek and Caryl Parry Jones.

6

Carwyn

There's no need for me to apologize here for turning my attention to the person I regarded as the most influential individual in rugby, the person who had the greatest influence on me as an individual, and whose influence can also be felt on Wales and its people. I first heard Carwyn's name at home, when my father used to mention him in the same breath as Cliff Morgan. He'd tell us, with pride, that he played against Carwyn in a match between Pontyberem and Cefneithin. He'd often mention Carwyn's exquisite side-step and skilful dummy. Carwyn would not only fool his opponents – a few of his own centres were fooled into thinking that they were getting a pass from him, before seeing him move in a totally different direction. According to my father, he was often breathtaking, and had an amazing ability to make time for himself, to set up for a perfect drop goal right between the posts. Carwyn went on to play for Llanelli, and Cliff Morgan went to Cardiff during the same period in the 1950s. This sparked a furious debate between east and west – which still happens in Welsh rugby today – about who was the better fly-half. Later, we saw the same thing happening with Barry John v David Watkins, Phil Bennett v Barry John, Gareth Davies v Phil Bennett, Malcolm Dacey v Gareth Davies, Neil Jenkins v Arwel Thomas – and I'm sure that other countries would love to have the blueprint for

One who had a great influence on me – Carwyn James.

Max Boyce's fly-half factory. But in the 1950s, Cliff Morgan was the first choice of the 'Big Five', with Carwyn having to be content with only two caps including one as a centre against France.

I first met Carwyn at Stradey during my final year at school, when many of us began training with the seven-a-side team, coached by Hywel Thomas. Because of his new post as Llanelli coach and his glittering career as a seven-a-side player, which included leading London Welsh to victory at Twickenham in the Middlesex Sevens, Carwyn would often attend the training sessions to share his advice and experience. I got to know him better when I played for the youth team at Stradey Park, and would often see him by the touchline during training sessions, giving us players his full attention. He felt that it was his duty, as club coach, to take notice of the youth team's development – and looking back at that time, it's interesting to see that many youth team members went on to become star players in the first team – players such as Phil Bennett, Hefin Jenkins, Gareth Jenkins, David Nicholas and others. One of the reasons for this was Carwyn's ability to nurture the development and confidence of players, having spotted their potential and raw talent.

It was during the summer training period before the beginning of the 1970 season that I had my first proper encounter with the master, and got to know him better. I soon realized that I was in the presence of a truly special individual, and a proud patriot who made no secret of his nationalist beliefs. More than anything, it was this that drew me to him, as I now had a stronger sense of Welsh patriotism, which had been stirred by Dafydd Iwan's songs. Before training or a match, I'd often be in the changing room, singing one of Dafydd Iwan's songs, when suddenly I'd hear Carwyn's light tenor voice joining in with just a few lines of the chorus. Occasionally, in his pre-match pep talk, he'd have a light-hearted dig at my singing, but would add a few sentences about the song to emphasise his personal point of view. As I said earlier, he never tried to hide his nationalistic views; indeed, he took them a few steps further by agreeing to be nominated as a

Plaid Cymru candidate for the General Election – in Llanelli of all places, a bastion of socialism. One of his opponents was Denzil Davies, who was a pupil at Carmarthen Gram when Carwyn taught there, but of more political relevance, Denzil had won the previous election with a majority of twenty-three thousand. Thinking back, I'm sure that Carwyn had no desire for a seat at Westminster, as he wasn't a professional politician by any means. Carwyn's nationalism was fuelled by emotion and his love of Welsh culture, and his main intention in standing for Llanelli was to raise awareness of Plaid Cymru so that it would be seen by the public as a viable political party. Even during his interview for the post of Lions coach in New Zealand, Carwyn couldn't resist the chance to emphasize that he was a Welshman first and foremost, and that he intended to stand for election, before inviting the panel of selectors to place their bets on the election outcome. The man from Cefneithin certainly had a sharp sense of humour.

After one match at Stradey, Carwyn came up to me and suggested that I should perhaps go to Carmarthen the following Sunday; a big Plaid Cymru event was being held at the old Lyric cinema, hosted by Gwynfor Evans and featuring some of the most popular Welsh performers of the time, such as Tony and Aloma. That was the first concert or public meeting I'd been to where the national anthem was

Four of Plaid Cymru's leading lights – Gwynfor Evans, Dafydd Iwan, Dafydd Elis Thomas and Dafydd Wigley.

sung at the end. I mentioned it to Carwyn at the training session the following Monday, and he was quite annoyed that I hadn't told him that I was there, as he would have invited me up on stage to stand with the hero who had won the

Carmarthen seat – the first ever seat for Plaid Cymru at Westminster. The fact that Carwyn said this came as a bit of a shock to me, to say the least, but it stoked the nationalist fire that was already burning in my subconscious. Although we belonged to different generations, these events brought us closer together.

In rugby, Carwyn was usually drawn to players with an element of genius and artistic flair, which meant that he responded more naturally to Barry John, J. J. Williams, Gerald Davies and Phil Bennett than to players who enjoyed nothing more than tackling and hurling themselves around the field. He was a person who preferred watching the prima donna rather than the chorus; yet, his thorough understanding of rugby enabled him to realize that the chorus was hugely important in allowing the 'stars' to accomplish their feats. To some extent,

Commentator and broadcaster David Parry Jones interviewing two who were instrumental in Llanelli's defeat of the All Blacks in 1972 – Delme and Carwyn.

Carwyn could look at a rugby team in cultural terms. Although the spotlight shone brighter on the ballet dancers – the backs – he knew full well that they would be nothing without the devotion of the rank and file. Carwyn's great strength was getting the rank and file to play well enough to set the stage for the star performers. He was a deep, sensitive man, who could appreciate the importance of every position, and on top of this, he had the skill of being able to deal with everybody, on and off the field, as individuals.

Carwyn's greatest quality was his rare ability to talk to everyone, from prime ministers to publicans and sinners, and make them feel totally at ease with him. This ability shone through whenever we went on tour or played an away game, because everywhere Carwyn went, he had a captive audience. And after the Lions tour in 1971, naturally enough, his audience grew. Despite this, I often felt that he was a lonely figure – always in the company of others, but also on his own, full of humour but also a sad and complex character. He loved analysing the team's performance after a match, and that analysis would be as accomplished as his analysis of a piece of literature or the prize-winning poems at the Eisteddfod. The way he analysed people and dealt with them accordingly was eye-opening. Having only just met a person, he could work out the best way of dealing with him or her. He never shouted at me from the touchline, and when I dropped the ball, or made a mess of things, his tenor voice would sing across the field – 'one hundred press-ups, Gravell' – and there would be nothing more than that. With others, his words would be sterner, and of course, his approach was perfect for always drawing the best out of players. Just before the kick-off, Carwyn would come to the changing room, especially before an important match, and give each player instructions, in a way that was private as well as public, so that each player felt that he'd been given a personal piece of advice. He'd then end it all with the words, 'Start thinking about the game, boys, it's a game for the mind as well as the body.'

It's impossible to measure something such as faith, but I'd say that every player at Stradey – and having spoken to some of the '71 Lions, it was the same for them – was ready to do anything that Carwyn asked them to. If Carwyn had told me to fly from one end of the field to the other, I'd be convinced that I had the ability to do it. Each one of us believed in everything he said, and after his great success with the Lions, our faith in him was even stronger. Having said that, the man was only flesh and blood, and when we relaxed with a few pints after a match, before the end of the evening, Carwyn would let his smooth tenor voice rise above the smoke, with a heartfelt rendition of the only song I ever heard him sing – '*Myfanwy*'. And he'd go through the song to the end, with his eyes shut tightly, having blocked everything else out of his own little world. On the field, however, he was the master, and our Gamaliel, who had an ability to identify each player's weakness on the field. Within a week or two after I started playing for the Llanelli team, he turned to me at the end of a training session, as we were leaving the field:

'Ray, what time do you finish work tomorrow night?'

'Half past four.'

'Right, I'll be here to meet you at five o'clock to practise your passing.'

He didn't ask whether I could come to Stradey by five o'clock, but rather stated his intention – and of course, I was there by five, with my rugby kit at the ready. We spent about forty-five minutes, with the help of some of the youth team, passing the ball from left to right, time and time again. This specific training went on for many weeks. Carwyn gave me his time and undivided attention, and we spent hours improving my individual game, and I can only thank that great man for his support and encouragement.

Carwyn was at the forefront of many administrative changes within Llanelli Rugby Club, and those changes were always beneficial for the players. He had a simple philosophy about this; if a crowd was paying money to see the players, the players themselves were the key element, and as a consequence, they had to be treated with respect. In the past, whenever Llanelli played against one of the big London teams, the team would travel from Llanelli by bus, early on Saturday morning, stopping for a sandwich or some sort of snack on the way. On Carwyn's insistence, the routine changed so that the team left by bus on Friday afternoon and stayed in a London hotel on Friday night, so that there was time for a decent meal and a chance to relax on Saturday morning. The players were often given the opportunity to stay for the Saturday night as well. If an additional training session was needed, which would make it impossible to leave before Saturday morning, we wouldn't have to spend hours travelling by bus – we'd travel by train, and get picked up by a bus from Paddington station. Players at the club were now afforded a higher status, and every squad member appreciated Carwyn's efforts to make everything more enjoyable for us.

Holding the ball in two hands to create uncertainty.

Fundamental changes were also made to the system of selecting the team – the decision was no longer left to a small committee: he was the coach, and therefore he had the strongest voice. The Club committee were wise enough to grant him that freedom, and of course, Carwyn was proved right: as an example of the club's consistently high standard, one only has to look at the results of the early 1970s, when the team reached the Welsh Cup final on five occasions.

Following his remarkable success in New Zealand and at Stradey, I know for a fact that Carwyn's great desire was to be given the opportunity to coach the national team – under the same terms and conditions, of course. Unfortunately, the game's administrators in Wales at the time weren't willing to bend the rules and constitution of the Welsh Rugby Union, and so his application for the post of Welsh coach was disregarded and deemed 'unconstitutional' by the conservative alickadoos. He knew full well that this would be the case, but he also knew that it was the only way that he could develop as a coach; on an international level, the Welsh Rugby Union missed a golden opportunity to break new ground. It was all a great disappointment to Carwyn, but later, after a period of working as a lecturer at Trinity College, Carmarthen, he had the opportunity to analyse the game as a journalist. Despite his love of words, I have a feeling that the process of writing felt like a penance for Carwyn, and that putting pen to paper was as painful as drawing blood. He was a vocal person, who brought insight and depth to sports coverage with his concise and constructive words. He had an amazing ability to assess the situation of a game in an instant, bringing a new dimension into commentary that hasn't been seen since in either Welsh or English. I've become more aware of that skill now, as I'm fortunate enough to be working in the media, but I'll never have Carwyn's vision and eloquence.

During 1972, preparations were well underway for the All Blacks' visit. Carwyn's main objective was to ensure victory for Llanelli against the might of the best team in the world. In 1971 he proved that even the greatest giants could be brought down, but that was achieved using the best creative talents ever seen in British rugby. He now faced a much greater challenge, to accomplish the same feat with a club team from a relatively small town in West Wales. As players, our faith in him grew even stronger, because from the very beginning he persuaded us that we had the ability to win, before slowly convincing each and every one of us that we were *going* to win. After all, Llanelli's record against international teams had been astounding over the preceding years, but in October 1972 the highest peak of all was yet to be conquered. And of course, Llanelli's greatest asset was its coach – a coach who had already proven, a year-and-a-half previously, that the All Blacks were only human. The months following the team's return from South Africa were filled with excitement, and that single match in October was arguably the only important match of the whole season. The chance to celebrate the club's centenary with a win against the All Blacks was eagerly anticipated under Delme Thomas's leadership.

Carwyn couldn't have coached any other club. It was here, at Stradey, that his first-class rugby career began, when he was still a Gwendraeth schoolboy. And wasn't it here, at Stradey, that he ended his career as a player in 1957 following a historic tour to Moscow for the World Festival of Youth Games? As a coach, he felt it was necessary to use the ball at every training

It was not only the Scarlets who thought him a master of the game. Just ask those Lions who toured New Zealand with him in 1971.

session, and that philosophy was used to great effect in New Zealand in 1971, according to Mike Gibson: 'Carwyn believed that the ball was essential if we were to develop the ability to handle the ball. . . He made us train very hard, but insisted that we always had the ball, and the more we played with the ball, the more it became an extension of our arms.' That philosophy ensured that I became a reasonably good passer, and also led, in the early 1970s, to the most exciting seasons ever seen at Stradey.

A photograph that says it all. Delme on cloud nine!

7

9 – 3

As the 1972/73 season drew near, all eyes were fixed on the last day of October – the momentous Tuesday which would see the Sosban team meet the wrath of the All Blacks.

In September and the beginning of October, I played about ten matches on the wing, and a few matches at centre. I must have created an impression on someone somewhere, as I was selected as a wing threequarter for the Wales B team in October (ten days before the big match at Stradey) in a match against France at the Arms Park. That was my first introduction to the fiery wing-forward, Jean Pierre Rives. But we ruled the roost that afternoon, and the French cockerels were beaten comparatively easily. My performance didn't set the world alight, but I did my bit.

Following the Lions' success in '71, Ray 'Chico' Hopkins decided to join us, along with Tommy David from Pontypridd and J. J. Williams from Bridgend. Their addition made the squad even stronger, as did the motivational leadership of Delme Thomas, the gentle giant. By now, there were three wingers at Stradey – Andy Hill, JJ and myself; at centre we had Roy Bergiers and Bernard Thomas;

and so I started worrying again about my place in the team. Was I a centre after all? Although Carwyn had said many times that a strong wing was necessary to face Bryan Williams of New Zealand, I was very reluctant to consider myself in that position – though I would have been prepared to play at hooker if necessary! In any case, during the last weeks of September, Bernard Thomas injured his knee, and after a while, the selectors were obliged to pick me as Roy's partner at centre – Roy having already played for Wales in the previous season. Bernard's misfortune ensured that I'd now get chosen for the team, and thus a new partnership began between Roy and me that proved very successful until Roy broke his leg and his career was brought to a premature end. The exercise and training started to intensify, with our focus fixed on the last day of October. On Monday evenings, we would no longer run on roads and sand dunes; rather, Carwyn and Norman arranged for one of the other west Wales teams to come to Stradey, and we'd play the likes of Kidwelly, Tumble and New Dock Stars. Norman was responsible for the forwards, while Carwyn dealt with us backs. On Wednesday nights, we'd usually have an official match, as well as on Saturday afternoons. Due to the pressure of this training programme, Carwyn wisely decided to invite other experienced coaches to take a few sessions at Stradey, which made the training different and fresh every time. Ray Williams came – he was the WRU's coaching organiser; Ieuan Evans returned too, who was one of Carwyn's predecessors at Stradey. These changes were carefully thought out by Carwyn, and they certainly succeeded in keeping us on our toes as a squad, with every coach using his strengths to bring the best out of players. Coaching methods in general have been criticized over the years, but in my opinion, when a club is fortunate enough to have a coach with a robust philosophy, it cannot be bettered, and this was definitely the case at Stradey in the early 1970s.

The week before the match, with Carwyn now lecturing at Trinity College, Carmarthen, the selectors – Carwyn, Norman, Delme and the chairman, Handel

Greville – met for lunch at the Ivy Bush Hotel in Carmarthen, and announced the Scarlets' team: Roger Davies, J. J. Williams, Roy Bergiers, Ray Gravell, Andy Hill, Phil Bennett, Ray Hopkins, Barry Llewelyn, Roy Thomas, Tony Crocker, Delme Thomas (captain), Derek Quinnell, Tom David, Hefin Jenkins and Gareth Jenkins. The only surprise or disappointment in their selection was that our regular scrum-half, Selwyn Williams, wasn't chosen, since Ray 'Chico' Hopkins had joined the squad. But there never was a better club member than good old Sel, and despite his disappointment, his commitment and enthusiasm as a squad member didn't falter. Long after 'Chico' left for the greener pastures of professional rugby, Sel remained a great asset to the club and became a firm favourite with the Stradey crowd. On the Saturday before the big match, we saw another sign of Carwyn's meticulousness as coach. The team and reserves were called to Stradey early that morning, where a bus awaited to take us to Gloucester to watch the All Blacks in their first match of the tour against the Western Counties. Although his personal organisational skills were poor, Carwyn insisted on perfect arrangements for his players at all times – lunch would be prepared for us in a hotel, before we went to watch the match. I had the chance to watch the giants from the far ends of the earth for the first time since my father took me to Stradey in 1963. Then, through a child's eye, the players seemed enormous, but at Gloucester on that Saturday afternoon – although they won the match easily and displayed remarkable skill – I realised that they were mere mortals, and that it *was* possible to beat them. On the bus on the way home along the south Wales coast, James the genius gave us a detailed and insightful analysis of the game. Looking back from the present, I'd be prepared to say that planning the trip that afternoon to the west of England was the greatest psychological aid that he gave us in all the preparations. On the journey home, Carwyn succeeded, not only to point out each player's strengths, but also held a magnifying glass to the main players' weaknesses. By the time we got back to the stand at Stradey Park, we were all feeling confident – it wasn't that we *could* beat the visitors, but that we *would* accomplish that feat. This was an example, yet again, of Carwyn's unique talent to create a bond between us, to make us have faith in each other on the field, and to make us believe in the words that he preached to us.

There was a buzz in the town and throughout every village in Dyfed about the match, which was spurred on by the endless facts in the press about the fearsome visitors. I must admit that the press coverage affected me too, because when the *Western Mail* published photographs of the visitors, I began studying my opponent's height and weight. Usually, if my opponent was quite big, I'd start worrying. But with time, I realized that I shouldn't believe every word I read in the papers – a few players turned out to be much smaller than expected

on the field! I knew, however, that a tough game lay ahead against New Zealand, and when the team was announced, I realized that it would be an unyielding and dangerous force to contend with. The following players had been selected: Joe Karam, Bryan Williams, Bruce Robertson, Mark Sayers, Duncan Hale, Bob Burgess, Lyn Colling, Keith Murdoch, Ron Urlich, Graham Whiting, Andy Haden, Peter Whiting, Alistair Scown, Alan Sutherland and Ian Kirkpatrick as captain.

I went to work as usual on Monday morning, but the workplace was buzzing with excitement for the following day. It was the same in the shops and on the streets – people looking for spare tickets, debating and predicting the outcome of the game – with anticipation spreading like wildfire through the neighbourhood. There was no escape from it – it was there at the dinner table, in my tea and bread-and-butter, the air that I breathed and even in my sleep. Looking back at my career, three definitive matches spring to mind – my first cap for Wales, my second cap (as I was playing at the Arms Park), and this match on October 31st, 1972. Until that week, I hadn't experienced anything like that electrifying, expectant atmosphere. To a fledgling player, it was beyond my comprehension. As each hour passed, the tension increased and my stomach began churning.

One of the main topics discussed during those final hours was, of course, the fact that New Zealand had returned to Llanelli to have some kind of revenge after being defeated by the Lions in 1971. The Lions' success was synonymous with Carwyn James's name, and as he was also Llanelli's coach, it was an opportunity to get him back by thrashing his club. That idea was at the forefront of everyone's minds (but I never found out whether or not it was true for the All Blacks themselves!) and this lent an extra edge to the anticipation. The players' response to this was to take it as another incentive to spur us on – as if we needed another incentive. One thing that should be said about Llanelli fans is that they're the most biased supporters you could find, and generally, they expect their club to be all-winning and all-conquering at Stradey. When that *doesn't* happen . . . well, it's not usually difficult to find a 'reason', which could be a blind referee, or a hurricane blowing in the team's direction during the second half. Saying that, the supporters appreciate a skilful and exciting performance by any team, and this has been demonstrated time and time again. And on this occasion, as on every other occasion, the staunch supporters were convinced that the Sosban would triumph on that Tuesday afternoon, and with a team that compared favourably with any other club team in the world, the supporters' faith was unwavering. Add to that the fact that Carwyn James was coach, and you have all the ingredients for a classic fairy tale or a 20th-century re-enactment of David and Goliath, played out on the field at Stradey.

Dawn broke on that Tuesday morning, and the players congregated at Stradey Park by half past ten. We were all deep in our thoughts as we stepped onto the Eynon's Trimsaran bus, which was waiting for us by the changing rooms, after we had placed our bags on the usual pegs. The bus then took us west, out of

Llanelli, towards Pwll and the Ashburnham Hotel and its renowned golf course. At the top table, the invited guests sat with the captain, Delme Thomas – and I'll never forget his lunch. I can see the waiter now, carrying a glass towards him, filled to the brim with sherry, before proceeding to crack two eggs into this glass. That, and nothing else, was his lunch. It reminded me of the times when Dad used to force me to swallow an egg cracked into a glass of milk; thinking about that slimy raw egg sliding down my throat still makes me feel nauseous. But there we go, Delme obviously had faith in that disgusting concoction.

During the lunch itself, Ray Williams from the Welsh Rugby Union said a few words, as well as the president and a few others, with a few words to finish from Carwyn himself. One of his memorable lines was: 'If you beat the All Blacks today, you'll become gods in this town. They'll remember you in a hundred years' time. After all, there will only be 15 of them, and we'll be 25,000!' Delme wasn't given a chance to speak – and I'm sure in my mind that Carwyn did this on purpose. He wanted to keep Delme's words back until the last minute in the changing room, as Delme was the only one allowed to speak there.

After lunch, the players and reserves were led to a separate room, where we had our final lecture from Carwyn. He spoke in detail about every position; starting with the full-back, Roger Davies, telling him to deal with the high balls; the two wingers were told to run and follow every ball, putting pressure on the visitors at every opportunity; Roy and I at centre were instructed to tackle and tackle, and if necessary, to tackle again, and it was suggested that I should show New Zealand's centres that there were harder men than them on the field; Phil and 'Chico' were told to kick very wide when the opportunity arose, so that the All Blacks full-back was forced to turn and run, and to turn him inside out if they could; each forward was reminded of his individual responsibility, and told to stay ahead of the game from the first kick to the final whistle; and the back row were urged to run and tackle and ensure second-phase possession, which would allow the backs to make good use of the ball. We would beat them at their own game. That, as always, was the theory, but very often, the theory doesn't translate very easily into practice.

With Carwyn's words ringing in our ears, we left the hotel and headed back to Stradey. There was only an hour-and-a-half till the match. I got on the bus and sat in the front seat; my mind drifted off and butterflies began fluttering in my stomach. When Delme got on, he sat next to me – the captain had obviously seen fear or panic or something else in my face. The next minute, he put a fatherly arm around my shoulder, and said, 'Don't worry about bugger all Gvav bach – everything will be OK, boy.' There were a few supporters around the Ashburnham, but when we began the journey, both sides of the road were full of people walking towards the field, a sea of red and white, each person waving a scarf or a flag as the bus passed by. It was an unforgettable experience. I'd never seen so many supporters walking from Pembrey and Pwll to a match at Stradey. I was part of something quite special – that was the only thing going through my mind; was it possible that this was something bigger than a game? I could now imagine how medieval warriors felt as they went into battle. Blood was racing through my veins, and I must admit that just thinking about those seconds has the same effect on me, even now. We then turned onto the road leading up to the big red gates, which was packed with supporters in red-and-white hats etc. I remember stepping off the bus, and heading straight for the changing room – and there, laid out neatly, was a new red shirt, new shorts and socks – the kit even had a special smell; it was the first time I wore a kit that was specially prepared for the club.

As the players started to get changed, an anxious Bert Peel turned up, and began putting plasters on any cuts and grazes, massaging any sore muscles and distributing pain killers for nagging headaches. Off he went, racing around the room, doing his best to keep every player happy and reasonably relaxed. There was just over half an hour to go, and I stood on the seat under the window, watching the crowd streaming into the field. I saw a few familiar faces in the crowd, but tried to avoid eye contact – I turned away, and focussed on Llanelli and the rest of the world entering Stradey Park. Someone said that the All Blacks had arrived on their bus, but I felt that it was too soon to look out for them on the field. Carwyn walked back and forth in his suit, cigarette always in hand, giving a few words of encouragement now and again. Nothing formal; he'd said everything that needed to be said and it was now up to us to perform. We had all the pieces of the puzzle, and for the next hour and a half it was a matter of bringing them together, with energy and dedication, to prove that Carwyn and Norman Gale's hard work had not been in vain.

I remember thinking that the next minutes were hell for us as players. They must have been twice as bad for Norman and Carwyn, who had made all the preparations, but had no control over the situation now. They could only sit back and watch – and try to have faith in the fifteen men that were about to go onto the field. Fifteen minutes to go, and everyone was asked to leave the changing room, apart from the team and Carwyn, as Delme – with his sleeves rolled up to his elbows, looking like a giant in the middle of the room – was waiting to begin his captain's speech. That was the most effective pep talk I ever heard during my whole career, including games for Wales, the Lions and the Barbarians. To be completely honest, I don't think that anyone of us could have handled another talk like that. It would have been too stressful. I'm not exaggerating. The giant stood, moving his gaze directly from one player to the next, aiming his words with the precision of an arrow. He didn't raise his voice at all; he didn't scream or shout. He whispered – an intense, incendiary whisper – and mentioned the things that were important to us as individuals: our families, wives or girlfriends, our friends and communities. He managed to bring a piece of Mynyddygarreg into the Llanelli changing room, just as he brought Phil Bennett a part of Felinfoel, and gave Roy Bergiers a piece of Carmarthen. In that comparatively small room on the last afternoon of October, he reminded us of all the things that were important to us in our own different ways. He focussed on each player individually, and by the time he got to me, tears were streaming down my face; Phil Bennett was crying too – the one and only time I saw him cry. The most important factor for me about those seconds was the honesty and the sincerity of Delme's words. He didn't ask us to do our best for the club or for his sake or Carwyn's – just for ourselves; in the afternoon ahead, we were to make the effort for our loved ones, and everything we cherished. If he'd asked us, we would have run through iron doors at his command. And then, ending the speech on a stirring note, Delme proclaimed that he'd return every cap he'd ever won for Wales and the Lions, if only he could have this one afternoon of joy. I don't doubt the sincerity of those words for a second. Two hours later, his attitude would possibly be different. But at that momentous second, as his speech reached its climax, there was a knock on the door, and the referee's voice, Mr Mike Titcombe from England, ordering us to join the New Zealanders on the pitch. Like the rest of the team, I was on fire; I had to reach the field as I was burning with enthusiasm; the door opened, and out we went through the little dark tunnel towards the pitch.

It was a cloudy afternoon, and as we reached the pitch, the only thing that struck me was the size of the crowd, and the vast areas of black either side. I'd seen many people arriving wearing red-and-white caps, but at that second, I saw nothing but a sea of faces and black shirts, and felt a wall of sound as we reached our theatre that afternoon. It was the Coliseum brought to life, in 20th-century Wales. During those few seconds, I was overwhelmed by a sense of fear, which completely surrounded me, and the only thing going through my mind was 'How can I get out of here?' For a short while, and for the only time in my life, I had an attack of claustrophobia. The visual aspect of the crowd was much more frightening than the noise, and I can't recall the minutes between stepping onto the pitch and the kick-off. I was shaken out of my panic by the referee's whistle at the beginning of the game, as we played towards the town end of the field, aiming for the scoreboard behind the posts.

The Llanelli team that defeated the All Blacks in 1972 – we all remember the XV on the pitch, but let us not forget the replacements: Back row (from the left) Selwyn Williams, Alan James, Chris Charles, Bryan Llewelyn. Front row: Gwyn Ashby and Meirion Davies.

Phil Bennett kicked off the match, and it was perfect. The ball seemed to be hovering in mid-air, waiting for Llanelli's forwards to reach it. I'd never seen Llanelli's forwards starting a match with such fervour, with Barry Llewelyn leading a fierce rush which demolished New Zealand's forwards. Carwyn's words were put into practice, and the pressure on the visitors was so intense that they were forced to infringe, which meant that the referee awarded us a penalty. Phil placed the ball some forty yards from the posts, and aimed; at the last second, the ball veered and hit the bar, before falling into the hands of the scrum-half, Lyn Colling. Before kicking the ball into touch, he paused – for a second too long. Roy and I were careering towards him at that very second. The ball was charged down over the line and Roy landed on it, scoring a vital try for Llanelli. The crowd exploded. Three minutes of play, and Llanelli were ahead – with two extra points to follow from Phil's conversion. 6-0. The back row ran in every direction, without giving the All Blacks' backs a second to defend themselves from the fleet of Scarlet shirts descending upon them. Delme Thomas made full use of his height in the lineouts, ensuring that the visitors had hardly any possession.

After twenty-five minutes, the All Blacks managed to enter Llanelli's half, and when one of our back row was caught off-side, Joe Karam, the New Zealand full-back, succeeded with a penalty from forty metres. 6-3, and from that point onwards, the match moved back and forth between the two twenty-twos, with Roy Thomas bridging the gaps on the blind side, Tommy David overpowering Alistair Scown, and 'Chico' Hopkins leaping around like a rubber ball ready to deal with both backs and forwards, and Roy and I in the middle, stemming endless waves of All Blacks. As the match progressed, we played with increasing confidence, while New Zealand's forwards became frustrated with our hold on the game. Keith Murdoch decided to give 'Chico' Hopkins a bit of a going over – but Gareth Jenkins wasn't prepared to let him have his own way. As a prize for his cavalier efforts, Gareth Jenkins was given the two blackest eyes I've ever seen – exactly like a panda. After half an hour of the second half, we had another penalty from the stand side, about fifty metres from the posts. Andy Hill, the extrovert winger and prolific scorer, aimed for goal, and before the kick reached its destination, Andy was already dancing a jig along the pitch. There was no chance of losing now. But defence was still important, and about four minutes before the end of the game, I had to bring Mark Sayers down with a hard tackle. The forwards rushed over us, with Keith Murdoch's foot making contact with my head once again, until I was nearly unconscious. I heard the referee's whistle, and realised that Murdoch was being penalised again, but I wasn't prepared for what happened next – that same referee started screaming in my ear, forcing me to get up, as there were only three minutes left of the match. My head was swimming, and my vision blurred, but suddenly the referee was helping me on my feet – he didn't want the match to go on for a second longer. I got up, in a daze, and carried on – though I had four stitches in my head at the end of the game.

The All Blacks lost the services of their winger, Bryan Williams, who was replaced by Grant Batty. Within seconds, Phil Bennett managed to make a fool of Batty. He caught a long kick from New Zealand, and side-stepped with such precision that Grant Batty was sent flying through the air, landing with a big belly flop. The crowd, of course, reacted to this incident and to Phil's skill in dealing with the situation – knowing that we were just about to make history. The fifteen of us realised that we only had a few seconds left; when another kick came from the visitors, Phil caught the ball once again and kicked it into touch.

Joe Karam at full tilt in the game between Llanelli and New Zealand in 1972.

I'm sure that the ball had already landed when Phil was struck by Alistair Scown's late tackle. He fell to the ground like a sack of potatoes and I was sure that he'd been badly injured. At that second, the final whistle was blown and Phil Bennett bounced to his feet – having miraculously recovered in a split second. I never saw him move so fast again. The place went wild, as we, the Llanelli team, tried to congratulate each other; some tried to reach out to the All Blacks to shake their hands, and thousands of Llanelli supporters tried to grab Delme Thomas to praise him, thank him, give him a knighthood – and whatever else they could do to him. In the end, he had to be carried off the pitch, with his muscular arms punching the air with joy. In the middle of this madness, a ten pound note was stuffed into Gareth Jenkins's hand as he fought his way off the field . . . with the generous businessman advising him to go to the nearest butcher to buy two steak fillets for his two black eyes!

The afternoon's greatest challenge was struggling through the crowd to get to the changing room, and finding that there were twice as many reporters there as there were players. That was the only time I saw Bleddyn Williams near the Stradey changing rooms. Champagne bottles appeared from somewhere (someone else must have had faith in us!), and with a glass of champagne in my hand, I stood still so that Bert Peel could start stitching my face back together. It took about an hour for things to calm down, before Carwyn James and Norman Gale could start congratulating us. If James released Excalibur from the stone in New Zealand in 1971, he crushed the stone to bits this time, and after getting changed and going for a drink in the players' room (both teams together), I was given an envelope, with the largest sum I'd ever received from the club – a huge amount of money at that time – ten pounds of 'beer money'. It was the first time I'd held a ten pound note – and there was not much of it left by the end of the evening! But the All Blacks were rather subdued that night; it's fair to say they'd had a huge disappointment. It hadn't crossed their minds for a second that they'd get beaten by a club team. Losing an international game on tour is hard

enough, but being beaten by a club team, in only the second match of the tour, was a very bitter pill to swallow. The dinner that evening was upstairs in the Stradey clubhouse, and I remember Ian Kirkpatrick making a fine after-dinner speech, as he cut a cake shaped like a rugby pitch: 'It's much easier to cut through this cake tonight than it was to cut through your defence this afternoon.' He was similar to Delme Thomas, in that he'd earned the respect of many players and supporters. But more importantly, both captains represented the best things about the game, by being honest and sincere, and by setting a good example to younger players. They were both strong, silent and dignified.

The rest of the New Zealand squad weren't too keen on socialising after their great disappointment, and returned quietly to their hotel for the evening. The same cannot be said for the Llanelli players and supporters; after all, didn't we drink the pubs dry?

120 tries in my career at Llanelli, and here's one of them – against Newport in the mid-1970s, with Gareth Jenkins and Dennis Davey in support. The open-mouthed referee with whistle poised is Ken Rowlands of Ynys-y-bŵl.

8

The Oval Globe

In November 1972, I never imagined that over the next twelve years I would have the opportunity to see Canada, the USA, the South Sea Islands, Hong Kong, Japan, Australia and South Africa, as well as nearly all of France and the British Isles. And all because I was quite good at chasing the oval ball. Playing rugby gave me great pleasure, but the travelling involved with it added another dimension that I never would have experienced if it weren't for the game, and that dimension was making friends and meeting people all over the world.

The remainder of the 1972/73 rugby season was unforgettable. As it was a special year, there was more interest than usual in the Welsh Cup competition, and we hoped to take it one step further than the previous season by bringing the cup to Stradey Park. The challenge began easily enough, but in the last sixteen, we were drawn to travel to Rhymney to face the local team. Rhymney should have been no obstacle to the team that had defeated New Zealand just a few months earlier!

But no one can take a cup-tie for granted, and Llanelli only just managed to reach the quarter-final, having struggled to beat Rhymney at the Memorial Park. In front of a crowd of over three thousand, Llanelli were losing 9-6, but with only a few minutes of the match left, Andy Hill crossed for a try that was converted by Phil Bennett. We scraped through 12-9. I missed that game because of an injury, and I could hardly believe the score when I read the *Sporting Post* that night. With that result, our hopes of reaching the final seemed highly unlikely, but we were drawn to face Bridgend in the last eight, which would be played at Stradey. Looking at Bridgend's record against us, we should have had a strong psychological advantage, as they'd only managed to beat us once at Stradey, and that was in 1950. I remember the game well, as it was the first time that a player was sent off in a cup match. The player dismissed by the referee, Meirion Joseph, was Bridgend's winger, Doug Schick, for a late tackle on Andy Hill, when the visitors were winning 3-0. From that incident onwards, there was only one team in the match, and in the end, Llanelli went through to the semi-final, 30-3, with the prospect of facing another black-shirted team – but it would be the Neath All-blacks this time, with the match being played at St Helen's in Swansea.

In the previous season's final, Neath's forwards gave us a proper hiding, and of course, that lesson was clear in our minds as we prepared for the match. A large crowd of around fifteen thousand turned up to watch, and once again, the pundits were predicting that the Neath forwards would take control of the match. For a while, this, indeed, was the case, but fortunately for us the All-blacks' dominance didn't translate into points, apart from a penalty from John Poole. But as Llanelli seemed to be losing their grip on the game, there came a much needed push from the forwards, with Tommy David displaying exceptional skill and power as he sprinted over the Neath try-line. And so, we were through to the final for the second consecutive season.

The preparations for the final against Cardiff on April 28th were extremely hard, and the press (the Cardiff press, of course!) were unanimous that only one team had a chance – and unsurprisingly, it wasn't Llanelli. To anyone from the west of Loughor Bridge, it was totally infuriating, and Carwyn James and Norman Gale began planning and preparing as thoroughly as they did before the New Zealand match back in October. This approach was taken out of pride, as winning the cup would be a fitting highlight to the club's centenary celebrations. A full training schedule was set, with the selectors wisely deciding to give the main players a rest every now and again in the weeks leading up to the match to keep up the squad's enthusiasm. Llanelli's record in matches against Cardiff was extremely poor – we'd only won one match in fourteen years – and this opportunity was not going to be squandered. Many feared that our forwards would be pushed off the Arms Park that afternoon, so Carwyn and Norman thought of a plan – they called on the services of R. H. Williams, the gigantic second row who'd been Welsh captain and a British Lion, and Howard 'Ash' Davies, a former Llanelli prop. A fortnight before the final, the team trained every night for a whole week, to prepare the scarlet army for any possible retaliation. Carwyn and Norman were like two generals, plotting a siege.

Saturday, April 28th, was a bright and beautiful spring day – the weather was perfect – and a crowd of over thirty thousand basked in the sunshine, ready to watch Llanelli having their inevitable beating. In reality, Delme Thomas and his fellow forwards were more than ready for battle, with the young prop Chris Charles back in the team after being sent off in a match against Neath. For reasons unknown to everyone apart from the Cardiff selectors, their strongest forward, Mike Knill, was left out of the squad, as well as their best kicker, the Welsh-speaker from Lampeter, John Davies. In the first half, the writing was on the wall for the capital city's team after Phil Bennett converted three penalties out of three, to which Cardiff responded with a solitary drop goal by Gareth Edwards. 9-3 at half-time, after Gareth Edwards had been prevented from crossing for a try by Llanelli's super-efficient back row. The anticipated superiority of Cardiff's forwards didn't materialise either, as Delme Thomas managed to leap higher than ever in the lineouts that afternoon. Our front row exerted complete control, and with Derek Quinnell a commanding presence, two or three men were needed to tackle him. Both teams' full-backs could have stayed in their changing rooms for the first half, as it was a personal battle between the forwards for the first forty minutes, with Selwyn Williams proving to be a serious challenge to the master, Gareth Edwards.

The pattern of the game changed completely in the second half after Phil's penalty kick bisected the posts from thirty yards. The forwards then dominated possession, and in one quick movement, the sprinting J.J. Williams got hold of the ball. He ran for twenty yards, before throwing the ball inside into my grasp when I was only a few yards from the line. I crossed it with two defenders hanging on my back. Needless to say, Phil converted the try, and went on to convert all seven kicks that afternoon. A try was scored by Cardiff's centre, Alex Finlayson, but by this time, Llanelli were in total control. And after a pass from Sel to Tommy David, a try was created for JJ, with Phil adding another two points. But the Sosban men weren't ready to rest on their laurels, and when Roy Bergiers tore through the Cardiff defence, Hefin Jenkins was on hand to cross for another try. Cardiff were comprehensively defeated 30-7.

Carwyn's words, in a post-match interview, gave a clear indication of his attitude – 'Preparation demands a positive mental attitude, and we decided to hold Cardiff's scrum, come what may. I've never seen our players so sharp at the end of a season.' He didn't say that the forwards would *try* or *attempt* to do this, but rather that they *would* hold their scrum. Delme held the cup high with pride at the Arms Park that April afternoon, with the cup on its way to Stradey in its centenary year. The spring sunshine brought a smile to the Llanelli team and their fans. There was also a feeling of vindication amongst those who remembered the Llanelli quartet who ventured to new pastures and joined

If there had been a Heineken Cup in the 1970s, Llanelli would have been the toast of Europe.

Cardiff at the end of the 1960s – Robert Morgan, D. Ken Jones, D. Brian Davies, and the unsurpassed Barry John. On top of this, winning that cup was just the beginning, as Llanelli would go on to win five finals in five years! We'd also succeeded by playing open, exciting and creative rugby – the culmination of ingenious coaching by men such as Ieuan Evans, Carwyn James and Norman Gale.

One of my fondest memories of the '73/74 season was getting to know the dear departed Bert Peel, Llanelli's physio or 'sponge man'. During my early days at Stradey, I remember Bert turning to me after one game and saying, 'Gravell, you're going to play for Wales one day, boy – you listen to what I'm telling you.' In a way, perhaps Bert's comment was partly responsible for making me decide to reach for that goal. One thing's for certain, I had total faith in Bert as a healer of injuries, and I spent many hours being treated by him at his home in Tumble. He was a witty man, with a story for all occasions. On tour, he was diplomatic but also friendly and outgoing, and enjoyed conversing with everyone, whatever their rank within the club. As well as that, through his travels and involvement with foreign teams, Bert did more to repair international relations than many a politician or diplomat. He was a person who lived life to the full, and was always beautifully turned out, with a silk handkerchief peeping out of his little jacket pocket. In no time, the old miner realized that I was a bit of a hypochondriac, always worrying about every cut and bruise. I can hear his voice now, preaching away – 'O, Gravell, boy, the problem's all in your head.' Despite this, he'd arrange for me to be treated in Tumble, where I'd always have a warm welcome from him and his wife, Rene. Bert had established his own injury treatment business, and people would be queuing up to be treated by him. He had to fit the business around his shifts at work, as he was also a foreman at Cwmgwili colliery, as well as being at Stradey for every match, and travelling to away games with the team. Bert loved sharing his memories about Dad and his colleagues at Pentre-mawr colliery. He knew them all because of Pentre-mawr's connection with Gwendraeth valley rugby clubs.

In one match against Moseley, I tackled Malcolm Swain (from the Swansea valley originally), and his studs tore my cheek quite badly. I had to leave the field just before half-time, and Bert supervised the process of repairing my cheek and chin with twelve stitches. Carwyn was the coach, and as he came into the treatment room at half-time, he didn't ask me to return to the game – he didn't even suggest it. All he said was that I was needed on the field. I didn't think twice. Out I went, with a plaster over the wound, and I managed to avoid many nasty collisions until about five minutes from the end, when I was at the receiving end of a high tackle, which opened the wound once again. Another job for Bert. The pain became even more agonising on the bus journey back to Llanelli when Bert started going through his repertoire of stories. I was trying my best not to laugh, but it was impossible, and as I laughed, two or three stitches came undone again. From then onwards, I used to say that Bert's jokes were different from everyone else's. Laughter makes my eyes water usually, but his jokes made my skin split open.

Another time, I had the dreaded 'dead leg' that is familiar to all players. At half-time, Bert massaged the leg with his skilful hands, and told me that the pain had gone. I then returned to the field, totally painless, before realising five minutes later that Bert had been treating my good leg! Talk about the healing power of words!

Bert's contribution to Llanelli Rugby Club was immeasurable, not only in terms of treating injuries, but also because he found a very efficient machine to clean the team's boots – and more importantly, he was a great representative for the club and Wales. I remember going to Bert a few times before matches, complaining of a terrible headache. Bert would nod his head, before opening his black bag, having a little rummage inside, and taking out a small dark bottle of pills. He'd give me two of them, with a stern warning that they were terribly strong and that I was to take them with water twenty minutes before the match. They must have been very effective pills, as my headaches always disappeared. A few years passed before I, and many other players, discovered that Bert used to buy pounds of Smarties and spent hours dividing the colours, and putting them into those little dark bottles that were intended to treat minor ailments.

The late and most dear Bert Peel healing the sick, Phil Bennett this time.

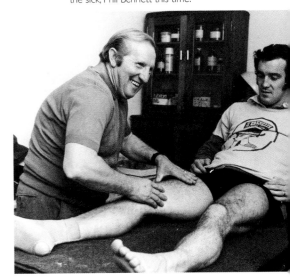

Faith is a great thing! Another incident from that year comes to mind. For some reason or other, I was working in the Tair-gwaith area, and had been suffering from a crick in my neck for some days, and the pain was getting worse. I looked for a kiosk to phone Bert. On the other end of the line, Bert listened to me moaning, before asking:

'Where are you now, Gravell?'

'In a kiosk, somewhere in Tairgwaith, Bert.'

'Turn left to look at the signpost, Gravell.'

Without thinking, I did just that, and felt another crick in my neck. Bert's voice was in my ear, asking,

'Well, Gravell, how is it now?'

Yes, Bert even had the ability to heal people over the phone!

There was something magical about Bert's sponge. Once, around Easter time, we were playing against a team of medical students from London at Stradey, and I brought their centre down with a hard tackle – so hard that he had to be treated by Bert. As he lay on the floor in agony, I was worried that he'd broken his leg, because when Bert arrived, the student was shouting, desperately trying to explain to him where the pain was.

'Where's the pain, boy, where's the pain?' Bert asked.

'My *rectus femorus*, my *rectus femorus*,' answered the student.

By now, I was convinced that he'd broken a bone, and went up to Bert and asked,

'Bert, shall I get a stretcher for him?'

'Stretcher? For God's sake, go and get a dictionary.'

Llanelli players represented the Cwmgwili colliery at the Miners' Gala Sevens many times, and we often won the competition, but we'd always play in our Llanelli shirts, with Bert as our team manager. But we were all there, really, to represent Bert. I've heard that Bert somehow managed to turn Barry John into 'Special Constable John' early on in his career, so that he could play a few games for Carmarthenshire Police! Yes, I did lose my temper with Bert more than once, for not taking my complaints seriously, but if Bert was here with us now, I'd be more than willing to admit, quietly – 'Bert, you were right, every time.' It was a pleasure to know him, and an honour to be considered a friend of his.

Back at Stradey, the cup competition began again, and as we were the reigning champions, everyone desperately wanted to beat Llanelli. In the first round, we scored freely and easily beating Glynneath 66-0. We faced a team from the same area in the second round, with an away-game against Crynant. It was an exceptionally hard game, but we won 14-9. Our next opponents were Cardiff High School Old Boys, and in the last eight, we went face to face with our first opponents from the first-class scene, Abertillery, and won again, 16-3. But in the semi-final, we had to face the mighty Pontypool, on the Talbot Athletic Ground at Aberavon. Over fifteen thousand supporters turned up to see the battle that afternoon, and it was a miracle that we won, as Pontypool's forwards tore us to shreds. Unfortunately, their full-back, Robin Williams, wasn't on top form, and he missed many penalty kicks. On the other hand, Delme scored a memorable try, and more importantly, Andy Hill's penalty kicks were spot on. We'd never felt so relieved to hear the final whistle than on that afternoon.

Andy Hill was our star player in the final too, against Aberavon on April 27th, 1974. He won the game for the Scarlets by 12-10. The Wizards, by the way, got the only try of the game. I should also point out that Phil Bennett, Roy Bergiers, J. J. Williams and Tommy David were absent from the team, as they'd been selected for the Lions' tour of South Africa. Therefore, put into context, the young team's performance in front of twenty-five thousand supporters was very commendable. Andy Hill should have received the Freedom of Llanelli, as he was struck on the head during the game, which made him see four posts instead of two when he lined up his kicks. Luckily, he chose the correct pair of posts every time! The cup stayed at Stradey for another year.

Sprinting like a greyhound to support a movement.

Following that season, we were all, apart from the Lions, looking forward to doing nothing for a month or two, before resuming our training to face the team from the South Seas, Tonga, in October. For a few days after winning the cup, I managed to forget everything about rugby, until I received an urgent message at work from Handel Greville. He'd received a phone call from the chairman of the Harlequins Rugby Club – a Trimsaran man originally, to my surprise – asking for some help to reinforce the team for a short tour to the south of France, to play two matches, against Pau and Toulouse. Because of various injuries, they were in need of a centre and a back row, which meant that I was invited, along with Gareth, Hefin Jenkins and Derek Quinnell. I knew, from my experience with the youth team and the B team, that the short tour would be hard work, but I was pleased, after accepting the invitation, to find myself in the centre with another guest player, Chris Wardlow from Northampton; I had a lot of respect for him, as he was a strong, hard player with a playing style similar to mine. The team captain was Earl Kirton, the former All Black outside-half, and from the minute I met him at Heathrow, he always had an orange in his right hand that he tossed into the air, and a copy of *The Times* under his other arm. The only time I saw him without the orange and *The Times* was on the pitch.

Everything had happened at short notice, and soon, the three of us were travelling to Heathrow to meet the Harlequins. Within minutes of joining them at the airport, I suffered a linguistic crisis. None of the Quins could understand the way I spoke, and their plummy accents – with words like *chaps* and *spiffing* – were hilarious to me. At the beginning, their attitude towards the game was very different too – they played for pure enjoyment. But when the match in Pau turned nasty, the Quins had to change their attitude pretty quickly. Toulouse were our next opponents on tour, with high-calibre players such as Rives, Villepreux, and Skrela, and in a break from tradition, both teams had their pre-match lunch at the same place. During the tour, I spent a lot of time with Earl Kirton, talking about similar experiences we'd had – I talked about Wales and the Welsh language, and he told me about the Maori and their traditions. I asked him many questions about the *Haka,* which is familiar to all those who follow the game, and was told that it used to be performed before the Maori went into battle. On the night of the match in Toulouse, we were all relaxing in one of the city's cafés, chatting to each other, with Earl Kirton still holding the orange in one hand, with *The Times* on the table in front of him. Earl was generally a very quiet person, but we'd all had a glass or two of the local wine. Suddenly, without warning and without saying a word, he got up from his chair and walked to the middle of the room. Off the field, that's the only time I remember seeing him without the orange in his hand! And then he started:

'*Haka mata . . .*'

The effect it had on the people in the café was breathtaking – exactly as if a line of dominoes had been knocked down; the silence moved from one table to the next, until the room was completely quiet, apart from the chant coming from Earl Kirton's lips. His face had completely changed, as if he'd been mentally transported from the bistro in Toulouse to Rotorua and the ceremonial battle preparations.

'*Haka mata, Kamata . . .*'

The silence was deafening, with Earl's chant building up to the *Haka*'s dramatic climax, as the five-foot-and-a-half outside-half reached the final cry with a leap that took him high off the ground. I sat there gobsmacked, taking everything in, feeling that Kirton was presenting something totally private to me personally. It was a thrilling performance, and after a few seconds of silence at the end, the applause began, loud enough to raise the roof. But seconds later, the wine was flowing again, and the orange back in the Maori's hand. I learned one thing that night – if you want some free wine, perform the *Haka*! I had such a thrill – as a Welshman, a nationalist, playing for a team that was the epitome of Englishness. I also came to the conclusion that it was alright to have the English as next-door neighbours, but living under the same roof as them was something else. We had so many differences, and the only thing we had in common was the game. And even then, our attitudes towards the game were worlds apart.

That summer, those of us involved with Llanelli Rugby Club enjoyed following the Lions' exploits, with thrilling film coverage of Phil Bennett and his crew on the rock-solid terrain of South Africa. We knew that the Lions from Stradey would not be able to play for some time after the tour, and that we'd begin the season without JJ, David, Bennett and Bergiers. One of the highlights was the match against Tonga at Stradey, and that evening a very promising number eight played for Llanelli – Phil Davies from Carmarthen – who lost his life a few years later in a terrible car crash. He had a great future ahead of him, which was cruelly cut short. I scored a try right underneath the posts that evening, but had to leave the field before the end of the match after a knock on the top of my head left me feeling dazed and confused. In the crowd that evening, there were two selectors – John Dawes and Keith Rowlands – and they both came to talk to me after the match, to tell me how much they'd enjoyed my contribution. I now had a real chance to wear Wales's red jersey.

9

Gwlad! Gwlad!

On Saturday afternoon, January 18th, 1975, I was at the rowdy coliseum of Parc des Princes in Paris, ready to confront one of the best rugby teams in the world.

If the noise was deafening when we stepped into the stadium, the kick-off caused it to double, then treble, until my head was spinning like a merry-go-round. A few minutes into the match, we threw to a lineout in our own half. Possession was won by Alan Martin, our second row, who gave the ball to the halfbacks – Gareth Edwards and John Bevan – who then passed it on to me. I managed to rush past the arms of the centre, Roland Bertranne, and released Steve Fenwick. In an instant, the phenomenal Gerald Davies was speeding over the line to score a try for Wales. What an unbelieveable start – but as with every game against France, their genius doesn't remain hidden for long, and soon enough, Jean-Pierre Lux, the left winger, was weaving his way through the middle for an excellent try. And from that second, we were all – inexperienced backs to some extent – fully aware that France, given enough possession, could do as they wished unless we tackled them firm and hard. With the speed of the game and the thunderous noise, it was impossible to think, as everything was happening at a frenetic pace. By half-time, we were still ahead, but we had forty

Destructive when necessary, but, remember, I could be creative also.

minutes left. Fatigue was our enemy now; it wasn't just physical exhaustion, but rather a combination of tension, emotion and noise, draining our energy. Because of our exhaustion, the French backs and forwards were throwing the ball around, with that inimitable panache of theirs, so that they had space to cross in the corner. But from somewhere – I've no idea where – John Bevan appeared (I accused him after the match of hiding in the stand until that moment!) to pull off the most crucial tackle of the game, not through brute force, but by artfully turning a Frenchman backwards over the touchline. That, perhaps, was the key moment. We realized that victory was possible!

The game was slowly coming to an end, with the French starting to run the ball towards us from every direction. That's their strength, and the most dangerous time to be up against them. Given freedom and space to move around, no other team in the world can beat them. We had to defend heroically. The French backs regained possession, with Bertranne trying to make a break in centre – I threw myself at him, and hit him so hard that the ball dropped from his hands. JJ appeared and kicked the ball up the field; two other kicks came from Geoff Wheel and JJ, before that giant of a prop, Graham Price, appeared like some Scarlet Pimpernel, winning the race to an unforgettable try. I still scratch my head and wonder how on earth did Price, all fifteen stone of him, manage to run at such speed at the end of a hard game. To those of you who've watched the try on *The Golden Years* video, you'll remember seeing Price, after scoring, throwing the ball into the air – but I don't remember the ball coming back to earth! The match was won 25-10. Champagne was flowing in the changing room, and I have a clear memory of sitting in the bath, with a glass of that beautiful golden drink in my hand. I must admit that I took ages to have a wash that afternoon, as I wanted to savour every minute of it. Quite literally, my cup was overflowing!

Then back on the bus to the Hotel Concorde, to get changed into a respectable dinner suit for the first time in my life; the jacket fitted perfectly, but the trousers were like something that Biggles would have worn in his adventure books, with plenty of room in the legs for two or three forwards! We then met in a private room, for a drink and a chat, and I told Cliff Jones that I hoped it wouldn't be the last time I'd play for Wales. With a smile spreading on his face, he answered that it was highly unlikely that they'd be making any changes to the team for the next match, adding,

'With the way you played today, Grav, you'll soon have a drawer full of caps.'

Ivor Jones then appeared from somewhere, a lifelong member of the Welsh Rugby Union, having played over five hundred matches for Llanelli, and considered a king in New Zealand long before Barry John was born. Ivor turned to me with a little black carrier bag in his hand:

'Gravell, you did well today.'

'Oh, thank you very much, Mr Jones,' – after all, he'd been one of Wales's selectors, years ago.

'Yes, very well, boy; and I can tell you now, I've put in a good word for you.'

'Oh, thank you again, Mr Jones.'

'Yes, indeed, I'm sure you'll have many caps. But listen, do me a little favour.'

'Right-o, Mr Jones, anything you say.'

'Here we are, then,' and he pulled out six copies of the match programme out of the carrier bag.

'I want to raffle these to raise money for Gorseinon hospital, but I need the autographs of every player and reserve from both teams on every copy. Could you do that for me?'

I spent the evening of the dinner wandering round the tables, getting autographs for Ivor. When I got home, and had a look at my personal programme, the only autographs I had were those of Geoff Wheel, JJ and my own. Ivor had his way! It was a pleasure to help him, but favours of that sort became a bit of a chore in a year or so, as I couldn't completely relax and enjoy myself with the others. And there was great fun to be had; I enjoyed the company, and listening to various speeches – some of which were interesting, others quite dull. But one of the disappointments I had was that no one gave a speech in Welsh after an international match. At that time, the Welsh Rugby Union felt no obligation to use the language, and I'm sure that any change to their conservative customs would have been unheard of. Today, it gives me great pleasure to hear the Welsh language having pride of place at the Millennium Stadium.

By now, I'd fulfilled one of my father's dreams ever since I began to show some promise with a rugby ball – which was representing Wales on the rugby field. But I knew that my success also made Mam proud, and perhaps there were a few tears of joy in her eyes on that Sunday afternoon, although Mam and I were sharing memories about another person, without ever mentioning his name. Of all the different shirts I wore during my career, this was the only one I kept to myself. I wouldn't sell it for all the money in the world! I saw other players' shirts being sold for unbelievable prices, for thousands of pounds, but I never allowed my shirts to be sold. Each one was presented to different rugby clubs, so that people could enjoy looking at them, but that first cap and shirt are completely priceless.

The second match of the season, two weeks later, was against England, and though the Paris match was my personal highlight, this match was just as exciting – my first match at the National Stadium, in front of our own supporters. This match has stayed in my mind for many reasons, and one of those is the fact that it was the only match that Mam came to see, without my knowing. Mam and Barbara, Dad's sister, were given tickets by Bryn Jones, the chemist from Pontyates – but no one said a word to me about this, as I wouldn't have been very happy to see Mam present. I knew that she'd get very worried if I had a nasty injury, and although she used to watch the games at home on the television, at least there she was in her own home, and that made me feel more at ease. I'm extremely proud that Mam had the chance to see me playing for Wales – though, if she'd asked me, I'm quite certain that I would have tried to talk her out of going.

Running out onto the field in Cardiff was an experience I've treasured ever since. In the years that followed, I had the chance to play for the Lions, the Barbarians and others, but nothing compared to this experience, and against the English of all people! If I was one of Glyndŵr's warriors in France, here I felt like a general with his army. I desperately wanted to play in that match, and one of the press reporters later confirmed that it was one of the best games I ever played during that period. I managed to pierce the English defence more than once, I didn't miss any tackles, and I'm quite certain that the fact we were playing against the English was partly responsible for my attitude that afternoon.

At the end of the match, I remember being invited for a quiet drink in Carwyn James's room in a hotel near the Angel. It was a joy to hear Carwyn's authoritative evaluation of the match. He gave a perceptive analysis of almost every movement, and focussed on a few of the good things I'd done during the game now and again. I still appreciate the lessons I learned from him; he had great teaching skills as well as a thorough knowledge of the game, which made it all very interesting but also coherent. That was the first time he concentrated on the good things I did in a game, and being praised by him gave me an enormous boost. As I left his room to go to the official dinner that evening, I was at least two feet taller. 'Ray, you proved yourself today against the English. You're here to stay in the red shirt.' Thank you Carwyn!

But all good things must come to an end, and within a few weeks, Scotland had their moment in the sun. They beat us in Edinburgh, and that defeat knocked us for six. Steve Fenwick and John Bevan were injured in the match, with Roger Blyth and Phil Bennett coming on as replacements. Those changes didn't help the situation, and in front of the largest crowd at Murrayfield for many years, the home team triumphed, deservedly. Very often, it's tempting to push failure to the back of the mind, but that match was different, as it led to my first proper encounter with Dafydd Iwan, though I'd listened to him hundreds of times and had seen him performing on stage in concerts. I spent a lot of time with him in Edinburgh, and that night, at the official dance, I taught the band to play '*Carlo*'. I then ventured in front of a crowd of players, committee members and fans, singing my heart out in the chorus '*Carlo'n whare polo gyda Dadi*' on the stage of the North British Hotel ballroom. Sometimes, meeting a hero can be very disappointing for many reasons, but meeting my hero, Dafydd Iwan, confirmed everything I thought of him. He was a warm, approachable person, and on top of that, he was a real livewire with a healthy sense of humour.

Despite the disappointing outcome of the match, it was a memorable night. There was now only one game left of my first season as an international player, and that would be against the Emerald Isle at the National Stadium in Cardiff. Poignantly, it would be Willie John McBride's last game. There were also two changes to the Welsh team since the beginning of the season: my Stradey colleague, Roy Bergiers, became my partner at centre, and another Stradey hero stepped in to replace the injured John Bevan, with Phil Bennett selected as outside-half. Another interesting fact is that there were three ex-pupils from one particular school wearing red shirts that afternoon; Roy and I at centre, and Gerald Davies on the wing, the three of us alumni of Queen Elizabeth School, Carmarthen – the Gram. It seems that it was a momentous occasion for the school too, as the children were all given a half-day because of us!

Every rugby match against Ireland tends to be ferocious and physically demanding; having said that, the Irish have a sense of humour, which transcends everything else, whatever the situation. Fifty million people across Europe were watching the match on their televisions, along with another fifty thousand at the Arms Park, all watching Wales monopolizing the game, winning with a cricket score. Wales dominated proceedings, as we managed to keep the ball away from Ireland's most gifted players, including Mike Gibson and Dick Milliken in midfield, and also prevented the Irish from taking control. Novices, like me, got a stern warning from experienced players before the match about the Irish command, 'Kick ahead, Oireland'. On one occasion, the ball was loose in midfield, and I was sprinting after it as fast as I could, when Willie John McBride's Northern Irish brogue was heard above all else, trying to egg on his team, which by now had lost all hope for victory – 'Kick ahead, Oireland, kick ahead, Oireland – any f....n head!' At that moment, we heard a combination of humour, despair and an admission from the Irish that they were being totally dominated by us. It was my first encounter with the Irish, and it turned into a close relationship as years went by. By now, nothing gives me more pleasure than crossing the Irish Sea, and experiencing a warm welcome and friendliness that I've yet to find anywhere else in the world.

Back at Stradey, however, the emphasis was on the Cup once again, and before Christmas in 1974, we scraped a victory at Taff's Well against the local team – the final score was 10-6. Following that match, I had my first television interview by Huw Llywelyn Davies, who had just joined Harlech Television as a reporter. I've no idea what he asked me, though! Then, we beat Amman United by over fifty points, before playing Pontypool, the week after the French game, at one of the most beautiful parks in Gwent. It was a memorable game too, in front of a crowd of over twenty thousand people, with JJ scoring a try after a quick interception. The tackling in this match was more ferocious than at Parc des Princes, and at the end of the game, Roy Bergiers's back looked as if it was covered with train tracks. An 18-9 victory for Llanelli, and an opportunity to play Bridgend in the semi-final at St Helen's on March 22nd. I'm afraid that only one team had a chance of winning that game, and that was the Scarlets – we won comprehensively 35-6. So, on Saturday April 26th, 1975, Llanelli featured in the final for the fourth consecutive season, aiming to win the cup for the third time.

Our opponents were Aberavon, who reached the National Stadium without conceding any tries to their opponents – quite an achievement in a hard competition like the Schweppes Cup. It was extremely hot – like midsummer – and Llanelli were favourites to win, even though we'd lost the services of an injured Derek Quinnell and Gareth Jenkins, who'd had seventeen stitches in his knee after falling on a brick in a match at Pontyates. The match was expected to be a battle between Aberavon's defence and Llanelli's creative attack. Adding an extra edge to it, Aberavon, naturally, wanted to get their own back for losing by just two points the previous year. Aberavon had already defeated Llanelli that season and were convinced that their forwards would deny our backs possession and give Llanelli a memorable thrashing. Unfortunately, no one told Llanelli's forwards that they were meant to lose the game! A crowd of over forty thousand turned up, in their shirt sleeves, to enjoy the spectacle of Llanelli completely demolishing the Aberavon pack, securing possession for try scorers Andy Hill, Phil Bennett and Tommy David. Then, Andy Hill topped it all off with a magnificent penalty kick from fifty yards. After the match, Phil Bennett said in a BBC interview: 'The heat was our greatest problem – but we certainly kept Aberavon's feet warm all afternoon!' The cup returned to Stradey for another year!

At the end of July 1975, we left the land of song for the land of *sake* and chopsticks, staying for a few days in Hong Kong, at the hotel where some scenes were filmed for the Peter Sellers film, *The Pink Panther*. On the second day of our stay in Hong Kong, I met a Welshwoman, Carys Gravell, from Aberystwyth, whose father, Jack Gravell, was originally from Mynyddygarreg. Think about it – I travelled to the ends of the earth and met a girl who not only had a connection with my little village, but was also related to me!

Carys was a teacher on the island of Hong Kong, and, for a few hours in the unbearably humid heat we created a little part of Wales in the Far East. The

Schweppes Cup Final, 1975 – Llanelli 15 Aberavon 6. This was our third cup victory in the 1970s.

Welsh summer of 1975 hadn't been particularly kind to us, so we all, inevitably, made the most of the chance to sunbathe in the wonderful sunshine – but some members of the squad paid very dearly for their sun worship. My nose turned as pink as the legendary Panther and was very painful, but it was nothing compared to poor Geoff Wheel, who burned his back so badly that he received urgent medical treatment and couldn't play any games at all in Hong Kong. In the match against Hong Kong, Geoff was responsible for the Welsh supporters in the stand. Lord Heycock and his wife were present at the match, and Geoff Wheel, with his superb diplomatic skills, told Lady Heycock that she couldn't sit in the Welsh squad's seats, with the immortal words, 'Heycock? I don't care if you're Allcock, you're not sitting there!'

Walking the streets of Hong Kong was quite an experience, with food stalls spilling over the pavements and the heady aroma of oriental spices filling the air. I did try a few different things, but I'm afraid that I've always been quite conservative when it comes to food, so thankfully I could have beef – a raw steak – for every meal. We then left Hong Kong, itself another memorable experience. The runway had been built out at sea because of the island's chronic lack of space, which meant that we could see boats and waves all around us as we looked through the plane windows. We charged along the runway – with such force that I held my breath until I felt the plane safely rising into the air, as I've never been a good swimmer! If everything felt strange and alien to me in Hong Kong, landing in Japan was an even greater shock, as its cultural differences were ten times more apparent – there seemed to be no western influences at all in the country. I was overwhelmed by everything around me – the people, the transport system, the buildings, and more than anything, the language. Very few Japanese people spoke English well enough to converse with us, which was very frustrating for me, as I love nothing more than good conversation. I had trouble getting used to the food too, with most meals consisting of raw fish, bowls of hot, dark soup and tons of boiled rice, inevitably followed by warm *sake*, Japan's national drink.

We stayed in Osaka for a few days, where the first test would be played. After living on bread-and-butter and coffee for a few days, I saw light at the end of the tunnel, when I found out that I could order steak in Japan too – excellent meat, bred in the Kobe region. Once again, having a beautiful thick steak in front of me brought a smile back to my face.

A massive crowd came to the luxurious stadium in Osaka to watch the first test on the Sunday afternoon, and my clearest memory of the match is that Mervyn Davies suffered severe burns on his back because of the substance put down by the Japanese to mark the field. They'd used raw lime, and the captain was in agonizing pain for days after the match. Before the kick-off, the Japanese manager and team members were confident that the team would do well against us, but Wales scored sixty points. That evening, as we walked into the official dinner in Osaka, we were surprised to find that Wales were the only team

The Welsh squad who toured Japan in 1975. The manager was Les Spence who had been a prisoner-of-war under the Japanese during the Second World War.

Steve Fenwick in open space in Japan.

Four Japanese encounters: (clockwise from top left) Yours truly with Phil and JPR miles behind! The late John Bevan of Aberavon looking to keep the ball alive. Graham Price, with ball in two hands, and JPR finding it easier to keep up! Geoff Wheel (second from right), legendary mauler and diplomat!

present in the magnificent dining room, with no one sitting at the tables set for the Japanese team. In his disappointment, Shiggy Kono, the manager, had sent home every team member in disgrace, feeling that their playing had been atrocious. Given the importance of discipline in Japanese culture, there was no forgiveness for the players; Shiggy Kono felt that they simply hadn't played to the best of their abilities. This was disappointing for us, as we never would have accused the Japanese team of complacency. The result could only really be attributed to our superiority.

We were treated like princes during our stay, with a visit to a little place in Osaka called Hakone, on the Shinkansen. We travelled on the amazing Japanese Bullet Train, going at a speed of over a hundred-and-forty miles an hour. From Hakone, we were taken to the foot of Mount Fuji, the holy mountain, which was surrounded by altars and temples to various gods, where many local people were solemnly carrying out their religious rituals. Leaving behind the astoundingly beautiful mountains, lakes and temples, we moved on to the capital city, Tokyo. After the peace and quiet of the countryside, the skyscrapers and congested traffic of the city came as a bit of a shock. The only time we managed to escape from the relentless hustle and bustle was during a visit to Emperor Hirohito's palace, when I was introduced to his granddaughter, Princess Shishibu. We all left that meeting with a brand new Seiko wristwatch, a keepsake of our visit to the Land of the Rising Sun.

In the second test, we were playing at the stadium where Lynn Davies won his long-jump gold medal at the 1964 Olympic Games. The stadium was now part of an enormous park, with thousands of acres dedicated to all kinds of sports, from baseball to Sumo wrestling. When the Japanese do something, there are no half measures – everything is done properly. However, the test match proved that we could also do everything properly – on the field, at least – with a score of eighty-eight points this time. Having said that, I sometimes felt that we were facing thirty opponents on the field, as they seemed to be tackling us in groups of three or four. They definitely put the effort in; unfortunately, they didn't have the necessary physical strength in the forwards to make it a fair contest. But at least we were joined by the Japanese team at the official dinner, as we enjoyed our final evening in the Far East. Despite the astounding beauty of the countryside surrounding Mount Fuji, I must admit that Japan wasn't one of my favourite countries; partly because of the total unfamiliarity of the language, which made communicating very difficult, and also the fact that I couldn't stomach the raw fish – *sushi* – or use chopsticks without making a terrible mess of myself and everything around me. I also didn't feel completely at ease in a country shaken by an earthquake every other day.

About a month after arriving back from Japan, I was offered a new job by Sharp and Fisher's. They were builders' merchants who happened to be looking for a rep in the Llanelli area to deal with customers, and of course, to look for new business opportunities. Like many commercial companies, they believed that having a famous face to promote their products would be good for business. The wage being offered was higher than my earnings at the Electricity Board, so I had to consider it and decided to take the job, as it also came with a bonus – a company car and telephone. Those material things were important to me at the time, though I soon realized that being a rep wasn't my true vocation, and that I wouldn't last too long in that field. In the end, I worked there for three years. I must say that the company was very good to me, but I'm sure that I was good for them too, as many of their customers were die-hard Llanelli fans. Because of that, selling things to them wasn't particularly difficult.

Within a few weeks of starting my job, anticipation was building for the touring Australian team's visit to Stradey on November 4th. A massive crowd turned up, but the atmosphere was nothing like that of the All Blacks' game back in '72. The match turned into a kicking contest between Phil Bennett of Llanelli and Paul McLean of Australia, which culminated in a draw, with both players scoring twenty points each. One of the strangest things about the game was that twenty-four points were scored in the first forty minutes. With only three minutes left of the match, Llanelli were ahead 28-25, when one red-bearded centre was caught off-side in front of the posts. McLean went on to convert the easiest penalty of the afternoon to secure a drawn match. The crowd left Stradey without being able to sing 'Who beat the Wallabies?' as 'good old Sosban Fach' had failed by a hair's breadth – or by the breadth of one Raymond Gravell's red beard! Within a few weeks, I was back in the Wales team once again, facing the Australians at the Arms Park – and this time, there would be no mistakes! The visitors were defeated quite easily, with J.J. Williams crossing for three tries, demonstrating his talent as a sprinter and an all-round attacker. Around Christmas time that year, I appeared for the first time with that very exclusive club, the Barbarians, when I was selected for their annual game against Leicester, and was also chosen for the second time to play Australia, as they

January 26, 1976 – The Barbarians 19 Australia 7. Nine Welshmen in the team – and I was honoured to partner Mike Gibson in midfield.

ended their tour with the traditional finale against the Barbarians at the Arms Park. It was a year of rugby honours for me, and I must admit that I was on top of the world. In terms of international games, the result of the match against Australia was a sign of things to come, as Wales won the Grand Slam in '75/76, in an extremely successful season where the victory against France at the National Stadium was the icing on the cake.

But I experienced another memorable event that season – which had nothing at all to do with rugby, but everything to do with my Welshness. On the night before the Scotland match, as was our custom before every game, the team and its officials went to a cinema in Cardiff, to relax and watch a film. That night, I knew that Dafydd Iwan was singing in a concert at the Reardon Smith Theatre in the city. That was where I wanted to be, rather than being stuck in a dark cinema watching a film that I didn't particularly want to see. So I went up to John Dawes, the Wales coach, and asked if I could be excused from the trip to the pictures. As I explained my reasons for wanting to be excused, he gave me a funny look for a minute, before granting permission for me to go, provided that I came back to the hotel by a certain time. Because of our dinner at the Angel, I arrived quite late at the theatre, but I slipped in quietly to the back of the auditorium to enjoy the rest of the concert, thinking that no one had seen me in the darkness. But Dafydd Iwan must have seen me getting into my seat, as he invited me to join him up on stage. I felt shy but also incredibly proud as I stepped towards the stage, and had an amazing response from the audience. I had to say a few words, and finished by singing '*Mae'n Wlad i Mi*' with Dafydd. I appreciated Dafydd's gesture, as he didn't have a particular reason for calling me up on stage. It was a thrill to share the platform with him.

The highlight of the rugby season was the opportunity to travel to the Emerald Isle for the second time, and having a chance to stay once again at the luxurious Shelbourne Hotel. Team visits to Ireland are very special because both teams stay in the same hotel, which means that a close relationship develops between members of both teams. It is a totally different experience from playing in other countries, and off the field, there's usually plenty of banter and natural friendliness. Wandering the streets of Dublin over the weekend was pure pleasure. The Irish accents were enchanting, and I enjoyed looking at the buildings and became more aware of the country's politics and history. If nothing else, those experiences strengthened my Welsh identity and nationalism, and made me think much more deeply about my Welsh heritage. It was no longer a superficial and emotional idea, or a feeling that came to life when I heard a Dafydd Iwan song, but rather a fundamental part of me. I now understood the meaning of Dr Gwynfor Evans's speeches, and Carwyn James's arguments. The visit to Dublin certainly stirred some deep emotions in me, and also developed my taste for Guinness – which of course, tastes completely different in Ireland.

The voice of Wales since the mid-1960s – Dafydd Iwan.

Back at Stradey, the campaign to keep the Welsh Cup in the glass case was hotting up, and once again, Llanelli had reached the final. It seemed that Stradey supporters felt that we had a divine right to get through to the final, and that other clubs should fight for the right to be our opponents. At least, that's how it seemed, with this being our fifth visit to the National Stadium in five years. Our excitement was tinged with sadness, however, due to Mervyn Davies's ill health, which eventually brought an end to his career. His difficulties began when he was playing in the semi-final between Swansea and Pontypool at the Arms Park. The crowd of fifteen thousand were completely unaware of the fact that Mervyn had suffered a brain haemorrhage, and that he was fighting for his life. It was a hard battle, which Mervyn gradually won, though rugby lost an exceptionally gifted player and an extremely capable captain of the Welsh team. Without doubt, he would have captained the Lions if it hadn't been for his illness. Without Mervyn, the final turned out to be pretty dull, with Llanelli easily winning the Cup, 16-4. Phil Bennett converted four penalties and J.J. Williams crossed for a crucial try; David Richards scored a try for Swansea. It was also the final match for one of Llanelli's long-serving players, Tony Crocker. But despite the disappointing game, the Schweppes Cup was on its way back down the M4, back to Stradey for the fourth consecutive year, and the totally biased supporters were thrilled with their victory against the Jacks.

After a summer without touring, I was ready and eager to face a new rugby season, and I still feel that I played my best rugby ever in 1976, between September and Christmas. But, the dream of representing the Lions out in New Zealand was shattered on Boxing Day, in the traditional match between Llanelli and London Welsh at Stradey. There was a week to go before the Welsh trial and I had complete confidence that I'd keep my place in the team. I made several breaks against the Exiles – I hurled myself into the visitors' twenty-two, pushing two of their forwards away before being tackled, and as I instinctively put the ball down, I felt a forceful kick on the side of my head. I knew I'd been injured when I felt something warm trickle down my chin and neck. Looking up, I saw Phil Bennett coming towards me, with the fear in his eyes contradicting his insistence that I'd only had a nasty little cut. Bert Peel came on the field, and confirmed this, saying 'Gravell, come off the field with me, so that I can stitch you up.'

I reached the treatment room, where Gareth Williams, the ENT specialist from Glangwili Hospital, was there to have a look at me. Gareth spent a long time stitching – it took eighteen stitches in all. He took a picture of the injury and tried to persuade me to take legal proceedings against the perpetrator; he was sure that the kick had been completely intentional. I didn't listen to him, as I thought that anything started on the rugby field should also end there. No forward or back is a saint, and although there's no room for behaviour like that in the game, I don't think that courts of law are the answer, but rather the clubs' own administrations. London Welsh knew full well who was responsible, which is usually the case when intentional injuries occur. Clubs should penalize those responsible, and even go so far as to ban players, which would make it a far cleaner game in my view. The occasional punch can't be stopped, as it's such a physical game, but individual clubs should be able to act to weed out the few psychopaths that wreak havoc behind the referee's back. I missed the final trial for Wales because of the stitches, but was selected to play against Ireland on the basis of my playing for Llanelli, and naturally, I was looking forward to the match at the National Stadium. On the Saturday before the match, Cardiff were Llanelli's opponents in an early round of the Cup, and I, like the last of the Mohicans, had a white band around my head to protect my ear, as many of the stitches were still there. Gareth Williams, fair play to him, could stitch as well as any Yves St Laurent.

Just before the end of the match, however, Gareth Edwards broke through the middle, and ran towards me. I decided to tackle him without much force, as both of us would be playing for Wales the following Saturday. Gareth, on the other hand, wasn't on the same wavelength as me, as he charged into me with all his might. Being relaxed and unprepared for the impact, I injured a nerve in my arm, and rather than facing the green shirts of Ireland, I found myself out of the game for over three months. I remember Gordon Rowley, the WRU's medical specialist, telling me that the change was psychosomatic. That was very distressing for me, as I didn't have the faintest idea what the word meant – perhaps I should have had a look at Bert Peel's dictionary! But psychological or not, the pain was intensely real to me, and I couldn't move my arm at all.

As well as missing the international season, the Lions were travelling to New Zealand that summer, and Delme had been talking for some time about his travels to the South Sea islands. He was certain that I'd have a warm welcome there, as I played the same style of rugby as they did. But no, it wasn't to be, although John Dawes tried to persuade me, as the season drew to an end, to play a few games for Llanelli to test my fitness. I didn't give in to the temptation, as I felt unable to give one hundred percent to the game.

My summers were always full, with endless invitations to open carnivals, summer fetes and prize-giving evenings, and the summer of '77 was fuller than usual with all the hard training. Although the requests took up all my spare time, I couldn't refuse those invitations; after all, I was being asked by my own community, and if people felt that I could be of some use to them, it was my duty to help them out as best I could. Those occasions caused me a bit of bother sometimes, as I've never been particularly organized. Off I went to open Penygroes carnival one afternoon, when I was meant to be opening another event in Llansteffan. Somehow or other, by a hair's breadth, I managed to be in the right place at the right time!

I was really looking forward to the start of the rugby season, and we had an important game during the first few weeks. Llanelli had travelled to the Brewery Field to play Bridgend, and I was back at centre with Roy Bergiers. From a personal point of view, if I had to choose the perfect match, this would be it. I opened up Bridgend's defence time and time again, creating three tries for Andy Hill on the wing. Some press reports were positively glowing. In *Y Faner*, Huw Llywelyn Davies wrote:

> I had a real thrill in the match . . . and that thrill was seeing Ray Gravell, Llanelli and Wales's colourful centre, back in the game, playing better than ever . . . Without doubt, from what we saw last Wednesday, Ray Gravell's exclusion from the Lions' squad was a great loss.

During that match I decided that I wanted to get my place back in the Wales team, and that no player was going to stop me that season. On September 10th, I found myself in the Barbarians' team at Twickenham, facing the Lions who'd been in New Zealand – a match to celebrate the Queen's silver jubilee! The occasion itself wasn't important to me at all, but the decision to play in an international arena was timely, and I relished the challenge of facing the Lions. My partner at centre was Dr Charles Kent, a giant of a man, with a pleasant personality as well as great talent on the rugby field. Gareth Edwards was at scrum-half, with David Richards as his partner, JPR was full-back and Gerald Davies on the wing. The Barbarians lost that Saturday afternoon, but as we left the field, Steve Fenwick worked his way towards me, to congratulate me on my performance (I created a try for JPR, and scored a try myself by charging past Derek Quinnell). He tried to persuade me to take his Lions shirt, saying, 'Ray, I'd like you to take this shirt, you should've had one over the summer.' I refused – even though I was deeply touched by his gesture. I felt that I'd only be entitled to wear a Lions shirt after playing for them myself.

By Christmas, I was ready to regain my place in the Welsh team, and the next step was creating a favourable impression in January's final trial. Gravell was on his way back, and with renewed physical strength, I pushed through to create a try for that little genius from Llan-saint, Gerald Davies. The partnership with Steve Fenwick also continued to run smoothly.

On February 4th, 1978, I got the chance to wear the Welsh shirt once again, at Twickenham against the old enemy. This was a special match – Gareth Edwards won his fiftieth cap for Wales, and the scrum-half had the honour of leading the team on to the field before we scraped through with a 9-6 victory, courtesy of Phil Bennett's three penalties. At the end of February, it was Scotland's turn to visit the Arms Park, and two things stay in my mind from that game: Aurona and I left our house on Friday afternoon, and got back the following Monday, after being snowed in on Saturday night. The second thing is that I crossed Scotland's line and scored my first try for Wales, and looking back, I could have crossed for three tries that afternoon. First of all, Gareth Edwards broke down the blindside, with me free outside him, but the powerful

An unforgettable day in February 1978. My first international try – against the Scots in Cardiff.

scrum-half fought his way over the line; then the try I managed to score from a quickly-taken free kick fifteen-yards from Scotland's try-line; and the third chance came in the second half when I made a break through the middle but decided to pass the ball to JPR rather than going for the line myself – a great mistake on my part, as it was a poor pass which the full-back failed to gather. It was a comfortable victory, however.

A fortnight later, we returned to Dublin, with the aim of winning the Triple Crown for the third consecutive time – a feat not previously accomplished by any British team. That was the most ferocious game I ever played; the pace was frenetic, the tackling terrifyingly hard, and the forwards were throwing themselves all over the place. At the end of the game, every player was exhausted, and could do nothing but sit down in the changing room. Cliff Jones came in and stood in the middle of the room, champagne bottle in hand, to make a speech:

> Boys, maybe you don't realise it now, but you'll understand the significance of this moment in years to come – you've made history. Something that's unlikely to be repeated ever again in the world of rugby.

There was one other hill to climb before the end of the season, and that was beating the French in Cardiff, and winning the Grand Slam for the fifth time since the war. It was a pleasant day in Cardiff, and I was woken by the bedside telephone ringing. The BBC were calling, from the programme *Sosban*, asking if I'd have a live chat on the programme with Richard Rees, who had two special guests in his Cardiff studio

– the brothers Dafydd Iwan and Huw Ceredig. I'm sure that I made history for a reason unrelated to rugby that day, as Radio Cymru broadcast a live duet on the programme, with one of the singers sitting on his hotel bed! Yes, Dafydd and I had to sing '*Ar Fryniau Bro Afallon*', and if I remember correctly, Dafydd was the one who forgot the words!

At lunch time, Carwyn James came to see me for a chat:

> Ray, if Wales are to win today, a lot depends on you and Steve at centre. You have to knock the French down in midfield, and if Phil kicks into to their twenty-two, it's essential that you keep the pressure on them all afternoon.

Carwyn wasn't coaching Wales or Llanelli at the time, but his advice was always welcome, and Steve Fenwick and I went out onto the field aiming to implement Carwyn's plan – and we succeeded too, as we won the Grand Slam once again, with some of the most exciting play seen at the National Stadium for a long time. This was achieved against one of the best teams to represent France for many a season. After twenty-five minutes, France were ahead 7-0, but our team spirit was so strong that we didn't concede any other points throughout the match. Gradually, we fought our way back with the half backs, Bennett and Edwards, beginning to display their authority, and the forwards striving for supremacy. Alan Martin heroically won possession at the lineouts, while the Pontypool front row were fulfilling Max Boyce's prophecy. From a scrum in France's twenty-two, Derek Quinnell passed the ball to Edwards, and Phil Bennett side-stepped through the mesmerized French defence for his first try. This was followed by Gareth Edwards's majestic drop goal after possession from the lineout. We then saw some ingenious touches by the scrum-half and winger, J.J. Williams, and a second try was scored by Phil Bennett, which put us ahead by 13-7 at half-time. In the second half, play moved frantically from one end of the field to the other, and the scoring reached its conclusion with Steve Fenwick's drop goal, which put us safely ahead.

We ended the season as champions, and following our success, the Grand Slam squad was invited to London. Unlike the honeymoon I spent with Aurona in London, this invitation included a visit to 10 Downing Street, where we met the Prime Minister James Callaghan. He was obviously quite knowledgeable about the game, and had been an avid follower of the Cardiff team. Thinking back about that evening, I'm sure that the wives enjoyed it more than us, as they had a chance to have a good look around Number Ten. The place was heaving as Mr and Mrs Callaghan welcomed us and, as someone said that evening, it would have been easier to get into the Arms Park on a match day without a ticket than getting into that political establishment.

The challenge of winning the '79 Grand Slam was ahead, but before then, the '78 champions had a gruelling summer ahead, far away from home in the land down under, Australia.

But inevitable changes were on the horizon. As celebrations were underway, before naming the squad for Australia, Gareth Edwards and Phil Bennett announced that they wouldn't be going. For Phil, it was partly due to his unpleasant experiences as Lions captain the previous summer. This was a big blow to the selectors, but it forced them to consider many promising young players – names such as Gareth Davies, Terry Holmes, Brynmor Williams, Alun Donovan and Pat Daniels, Stuart Lane, Clive Davies, John Richardson and Mike Watkins. The general consensus was that the Welsh-speaker from Cardigan, Brynmor Williams, would probably step into Gareth Edwards's boots. That, indeed, was the case: he won his first cap in the first test against Brisbane. But another young boy, Terry Holmes, was hot on his heels from the beginning.

The tour began with a match against Western Australia in Perth, and although the team didn't dazzle, we easily managed to score thirty-two points. We then moved on to Melbourne, and within a few hours of arriving, my

All ready for Australia in 1978 – both tests were lost but Wales were hard done by as a result of the opposition's deplorable attitude and some weak refereeing.

temperature soared. I felt awful, and following a medical examination, I was told that I had 'Melbourne Flu'. Flu or no flu, I had to try playing to have a taste of Australian rugby, and so we played against Victoria Province, scoring fifty-two points in the process.

From the city of Melbourne, the rugby squad moved on to Sydney, to play that city's team – and we lost, for the first time, 16-18. We stayed in a posh hotel at Rushcutters Bay, where we met the famous cricketer Tony Greig, who was busily making his fortune appearing in a breakfast cereal advert; he was quite a modest person, and great company too. We left Sydney then, to play the rural team of New South Wales, in a little town called Cobar. I remember hurting my leg during that game – what we'd call a dead leg, but the Australians referred to it as a 'corked leg'. Back in Sydney, my leg received daily treatment in a city clinic, under the supervision of Dr Syd Sugarman. By the following Saturday, my condition had improved enough for me to take my place in the team against New South Wales, before travelling to Ballymore, Brisbane, to play against Queensland, where I met my old friend, Jeff Shaw. After the match, I was introduced to the most diabolical drink I've ever had, which was Binderberg Rum. It had a diabolical effect on me too – Terry Cobner found me in the lift in the early hours of the morning, arguing with the door! J.P.R. Williams shared the drink with me, and the next morning, it could be said that the full-back and centre were feeling slightly worse for wear!

On the Sunday before the first test in Brisbane, I felt real fear for the first time in a rugby match, and it hit me before the game even began. The centres for Australia were Andrew Slack, winning his first cap, and Martin Knight, who was quite experienced. I'd never met the latter before that match, but as we crossed from one side of the field to the other to prepare for the kick-off, I felt a hard blow on the side of my head. Everything blacked out for a few seconds, but I snapped out of my daze, got down on my knees in the middle of the field, and tried to get my head together. Mr Knight had made his presence felt in the most vicious way possible; I felt absolutely terrified before kick-off. There I was, trying to clear my head – in agony both physically and mentally – with Steve Fenwick's hand dragging me to my feet by my shirt collar. I had two choices – either to accept what had happened, which meant conceding the psychological advantage straight away, or to react in a totally primitive and physical way. In the opening minutes, Paul McLean, Australia's outside-half, put up a high ball towards Wales's posts, with Knight in hot pursuit. As Knight chased it with all his might, I went straight for him and floored him. Thinking about my decision and that incident doesn't give me an ounce of pleasure now, but at that moment, I had to fight fire with fire, and the heat was on for the remainder of those eighty minutes. One of Australia's forwards kicked Terry Cobner's head on purpose – a kick that could have cost him his life. It's no exaggeration that this was the dirtiest play I ever saw on a rugby field. Wales's players were no angels, but I never saw anything like the Australians' attitude, and the referee seemed to be turning a blind eye to all the foul play. I must admit that I was quite relieved to hear the final whistle. The Welsh players' injuries were so severe that the changing room looked more like a field hospital.

A week later, the second test was played at Sydney's famous cricket ground, and because of the injuries, the Welsh team seemed strangely unfamiliar – Gerald Davies was captain in Cobner's absence; Stuart Lane, Clive Davies and J.P.R. Williams playing in the back row and young Terry Holmes winning his first cap for his country. The Swansea valley boy, Alun Donovan, was the full-back. The home team won, with one conversion that was at least two feet outside the posts. During the match, Steve Finnane hit Graham Price with an incredibly cowardly punch, when Price's back was turned to him. It was obviously a premeditated attack, but the referee did nothing about the incident, despite the fact that Graham Price had to leave the field in excruciating pain. This act was enough to make each one of us feel physically sick, and the image I have of Price, leaving the field with a bloodied face, is a very vivid example of rugby's worst aspects. In the post-match dinner, the manager, Clive Rowlands, was strong and brave enough to make a speech that was very critical of Finnane's behaviour, and I have great respect for Clive for what he did. He voiced his opinion in public there and then, rather than waiting until we got home, twelve thousand miles away. Graham Price refused treatment in Sydney that night, and insisted on travelling home with the rest of the team the next morning. For once in his life, he was silent – he couldn't say a word as his chin was bandaged up! After the warm welcome we received off the field in Australia, it's a shame that the tour finished on such a sour note – the bitterness stayed with us for some time.

That summer – the summer of the Australian massacre – I changed my job once again. I didn't feel that my future lay in sales and marketing, but there weren't many job opportunities, and so I joined Memcem, a company that J.J.

In the West Wales shirt at St Helen's, 1978.

Williams worked for at the time. My job was still in sales – but this time I was selling chemicals to clean factories and buildings, and although I was better paid and had an impressive car, it was the most boring period I ever spent in employment. Every day in the job confirmed my suspicions that I'd never be a good salesperson. I only stayed in the job for ten months, but they felt like very long months as I tried my best to sell products that I had no interest in, whatsoever. In September, I went back to Stradey, anticipating a successful season for Llanelli and Wales, and of course, I was looking forward to another visit from New Zealand's giants.

Clive Rowlands was chosen as the West Wales coach to prepare for the All Blacks match on October 25th, and I found myself with my good friend Roy Bergiers once again at centre. The team seemed strong, and over forty thousand came to see us flying the flag in Swansea. By the final whistle, the flag was quite limp, as we were no match for the visitors' strength, who gave us a painful hiding, 23-7. One section of the crowd blamed the referee for some strange decisions, but he had nothing to do with the final result. Our only response to the All Blacks' endless scoring was one try by Roy Bergiers and a penalty kick by Roger Blyth. The All Blacks managed to cross for three tries; one for Gary Knight and two for the speedy winger, Stu Wilson.

The Welsh team was announced at the end of October, and there were a few raised eyebrows when some of the names were announced. The captain would be John Peter Rhys Williams, with the builder from Aberporth, Paul Ringer, in the back row.

On November 11th, at five to four in the afternoon, Brian McKechnie kicked a fateful kick for the All Blacks after the referee Roger Quittenton penalised Geoff Wheel for pushing in a lineout on Wales's ten-yard line. Millions of television viewers saw the event time and time again – Andy Haden from New Zealand flying from the line without a Welshman near him, and the referee's arm shooting to the air to indicate a penalty. The questioning began later when reporters went looking for Haden everywhere, and were told by the manager, Russ Thomas, that the experienced second row was ill in bed with glandular fever! The visitors' cheating had brought them victory right under our noses. This was admitted many times later, but, at the time, there was no apology. I'm sure that they felt it was a chance to get their own back, for what happened in 1905!

This big drama was headline news for days, but in the meantime at my own club, another storm was brewing. The previous week, Chris Ralston had been seriously injured in the match between Llanelli and Richmond, and had received over thirty stitches to a wound on his head. This story developed into front page news, and the Llanelli Rugby Club committee were urged to find the perpetrator. He wasn't named, but the club was brave enough to suspend the pack who played in that match against Richmond, and named eight different forwards for the match against Swansea the following Tuesday after the international match. The incident was very damaging to the club, especially as Llanelli had always been considered a club that strived to play rugby with flair, and had no previous history of dirty play. There was a dark cloud above Stradey for many months after that, and we had to endure quite a hostile response from many crowds, especially over the border in England. Indeed, at the beginning of

December, our scrum-half, Vernon Richards, was sent off at Northampton after being accused – a totally groundless accusation – of putting the boot in. Ralston's injury was the reason for this decision and for the crowd's hostility, especially as Llanelli had been unable to name and shame the guilty player. At the beginning of the New Year, I was back in the Wales team to play the first match in Scotland. At last, Elgan Rees got his first full cap – he'd represented the Lions before wearing his country's red shirt. The season began triumphantly at Murrayfield, and there were no changes at all to the team for the second match in Cardiff against England. This match was full of mistakes, from both sides, but it ended in victory for Wales 24-20. The press were rather unkind – I was criticized for cutting back in too often, and J.J. Williams was a villain for not being creative enough. But yet again, according to John Dawes, 'It would be unfair to blame our backs as they were only given poor possession.'

When the team was announced to play France, I was travelling in my car and listening eagerly to John Evans announcing that there would only be one change to the team. 'Damn them,' I said, 'they've left out Terry Holmes.' 'David Richards is at centre instead of Ray Gravell,' said John Evans. I cried like a baby, and felt as if the world was falling apart around me. Wasn't life cruel? Here they were, announcing the team, without even letting me know that I'd been left out. Many years later I realized that I had no right to expect any different. After all, wasn't I in my car when I heard that I'd been awarded my first cap?

10

The Lion

In April 1980, I was elected captain of Llanelli Rugby Club for the 1980/81 season, ten years after wearing the scarlet shirt for the first time. For me, this honour was second only to the honour of representing Wales, and it was followed, a few days later, by a phone call from Marlston Morgan to say that I was also in the Lions squad. My cup was overflowing – literally, as I was invited by Marlston to share a bottle of champagne with him in his office to celebrate the news. It's no surprise that the Lions tour in 1980, like the team itself, was considered a failure, as the series against South Africa was lost. The tour was plagued by injuries, and everything could have been very different. But I'll go back to the beginning, to May 3rd, when thirty players from all over Britain and Ireland met at Heathrow Airport. They would be spending ten weeks of their lives in one of the most complicated countries in the world – which I personally would be visiting for the third time. A country full of fear, tension and anger, due to its apartheid regime. And although many players expressed their abhorrence of that regime, none of us would have chosen to miss the tour.

Realising another dream: playing for the Lions in a test match in South Africa in 1980.

There was strong opposition to sporting tours to this vast country on the African continent. Politically, in Britain and in Europe, an increasing number of parties and individuals were expressing the opinion that the only way to resolve the injustice in South Africa was *to have nothing to do with them*. In Wales, people were refusing to buy grapes and wine from the Cape, and letting Outspan oranges rot on the shelves and joining the anti-apartheid movement that was building momentum. Why then, did I tour a country that had been subjecting black people to terrible physical and mental abuse for years?

I was a rugby player, who spent every minute of the day focussing completely on perfecting my skill and technique in order to reach the top. I was, to all intents and purposes, a 'professional' player, some twenty years before Vernon Pugh and his committee changed the game's direction. Selfish? . . . Possibly, but at least I'll admit to it.

I, Raymond Gravell from the village of Mynyddygarreg, was comfortable with people of all backgrounds – my upbringing in the Gwendraeth valley was responsible for that. People are people. I was well aware of the contempt shown to the black people of South Africa; I knew that they lived in terrible conditions that were totally unacceptable – after all, I'd seen the shanty towns (that had no amenities such as electricity, water and sewerage) as I travelled across the country. The presence of black people in our matches was proof of their feelings – loudly supporting us rather than the Springboks! Although I was a naïve young man, I began to realise that there was a desperate need for change in the country to ensure justice and fair play for all.

Travelling to the other ends of the earth opened my eyes and challenged many of my beliefs – let us be honest and admit that the Aborigine in Australia and the Maori in New Zealand are abused, and are usually treated as second-class citizens. My duty was to play rugby, and let the authorities fight for change in the political system. The apartheid regime in South Africa was brought down by the heroism of Nelson Mandela and his army of colleagues. A personal protest from Raymond Gravell wouldn't have helped their fight – because I still believe that keeping in contact and having a quiet influence can be effective.

The squad was comprised of twelve Welshmen, eight Englishmen, five Scots and five Irishmen, and the captain, Bill Beaumont, was the first Englishman to lead the Lions for fifty years. The response of the public and media was positive, compared to the situation back home, six thousand miles away, as South Africa's selectors named six black players amongst the sixty chosen for the tests. It seemed to be a bit of a token gesture, with the country's rugby authorities making a conscious effort to prove that the game was becoming multi-racial. But three black players were undoubtedly there because of their immense talent, namely Hennie Shields, the centre, Nicky Davids on the wing, and the talented outside-half, Errol Tobias who played at Stradey for the South African Barbarians.

Upon our arrival at Jan Smuts airport, Johannesburg, we were greeted by hundreds of supporters before being taken to Vanderbijlpark, an industrial town some forty miles south of Johannesburg. Within a few hours of arriving at the hotel, the coach, Noel Murphy, and the manager, Syd Millar, were pushing us through an hour of intense training under the scorching sun. It was an hour of pure hell, with air so thin that it made breathing difficult; the hard terrain was causing blisters to erupt on our feet. On top of that, I had severe sunburn on my nose again – I was christened Rudolph for a while! I'd have two English newspapers in my room every morning, and even the front pages would be filled with pictures of us training, eating and smiling; but other papers, especially those intended for black people, didn't mention the Lions at all. In the hotel, there were rows of black waiters to cater for our every need, and I'd share a few cans of beer with them. After a few days of hard training, there came a chance to visit the Sharpeville township, the scene of a terrible conflict twenty years previously. Alongside this place, there were endless rows of one-storey houses, over six thousand of them, without water or electricity or amenities, and within seconds we were surrounded by dozens of children.

Things started to go awry in the first match. Although we won, in terms of points, we lost the services of two players – Stuart Lane, with an injured knee, and Gareth Davies who'd dislocated his shoulder. Lane had to go home, and a reserve was requested to travel out to replace him. During the first weeks, we heard one name mentioned over and over, that of Naas Botha, South Africa's talented outside-half, who could kick a ball over sixty metres, without fail. It was obvious that Botha would become a thorn in our flesh in the test matches.

The 1980 Lion going hell for leather for the try-line.

The injuries were still causing concern, as Phil Blakeway, our prop, broke his ribs, and then Ollie Campbell pulled a hamstring. Just as Gareth Williams was travelling from Bridgend to join us, Syd Millar recruited Welshman Ian Stephens, and Irishman Tony Ward as replacements for Blakeway and Campbell. In the match on May 21st against the Select XV, one of rugby football's greatest tries was scored in a movement that ran continuously for almost a minute-and-a-half, with the ball being handled by thirty-two pairs of hands. As Derek Quinnell said after the match, 'The fifteen of us scored that try.' But playing on fields that were at least one thousand feet above Snowdon was strenuous, and after only twenty minutes, I was down on my knees. I took my hat off to the forwards, as they had to fight for the ball as well as run around the field. It's the only country where altitude must be considered when planning a rugby tour. It would have been much easier for us to play every highland game consecutively, so that we could have acclimatized to our surroundings and the thin air – but it's unlikely that the South African coaches would have agreed to that. In Stellenbosch, at the impressive Danie Craven Stadium, we were besieged by more problems, when Fran Cotton was led off the field, suffering from chest pains. Fran was rushed straight away to the University Hospital, and everyone started worrying that he'd had a heart attack. The next day, he was transferred to Groote Schuur hospital in Cape Town, where he was placed in intensive care for thorough examinations. A few days later, it was a great relief to everyone that he hadn't had a heart attack, but rather that he suffered from an illness called pericarditis.

So, from the original squad that left Heathrow, we had lost seven players, and when the time came to select the team for the first test, only one pair of halfbacks was available. By half-time, Naas Botha had confirmed the rumours we'd heard about his playing, and had put South Africa ahead 16-9. I was a replacement in this match, but had to go onto the field in the second half when John Carleton injured his ribs. Tony Ward managed to bring the score up to 16-12 with a fourth penalty kick. Later, Graham Price crossed over for a try, bringing the scores level, and then Ward again converted, putting us ahead for the first time in the match, 19-16. But South Africa got the better of us, scoring two tries in the final minutes. The final score was 26–22.

After that result, the squad felt quite miserable, but more bad news was to come when the squad's best winger, Mike Slemen, returned home due to a family illness. We were halfway through the tour by now, and Slemen's replacement, Andy Irvine, having played one match against Transvaal in Johannesburg, was selected as full-back for the second test at Bloemfontein; Gareth Davies had returned at outside-half. We lost Terry Holmes in the match against Transvaal, with a serious knee injury – a problem that would plague him for the rest of his career.

The ball tucked away safely as I hand off a Western Province centre.

Going into the second test, the Lions had played ten matches, and had only lost the first test. On a sunny June day, a crowd of sixty thousand people were eagerly waiting for their heroes to triumph again, and just like the first test, South Africa shot ahead 16-9 at half-time. Gareth Davies's penalty kicks closed the gap to one point, but the outside-half had to leave the field after injuring his knee. John O'Driscoll, on the other hand, was playing the match of his life, and was a constant thorn in our opponents' flesh. He was a very likeable man, and we became close friends during the tour. In the second half of the test, I was struck on the nape by Plessis, and I passed out for a few minutes. The doctors, Jack Matthews and John O'Driscoll, examined me on the field, and when I came-to, the only thing I could remember was that I was in South Africa; I had no idea of the score. O'Driscoll tried to persuade me to leave the field, but I refused. I insisted on staying, despite the fact that I was in a complete daze for fifteen minutes – and O'Driscoll had a few stern words with me after the match for not heeding his advice. South Africa were in complete control for a long time before I managed to cross for a try in the final seconds after receiving a pass from Clive Woodward – which made the score somewhat more respectable. It was the same story at the Port Elizabeth test – losing by two points (12–10) although we had plenty of opportunities to gain control. Once again, Botha impressed us all in the match with a conversion, a penalty and a drop goal.

The tour was now drawing to an end, and everyone's thoughts turned homewards; only three games were left before the final test. Although we lost the first three tests, it was important that we remained unbeaten in every regional and provincial match, and try to end on a high note. Following victories against the Barbarians, Western Province and Griqualand West, it was announced that Bill Beaumont's Lions were only the second team ever to win every provincial game, which raised our spirits even though the injuries were still mounting, with scrum-half Colin Patterson also taken to hospital.

The following Saturday, the eighteenth match of the tour, we had to face the might of South Africa and prevent them from claiming a series whitewash. The forwards remained heroic throughout the tour, but we didn't always make the best use of our possession. Could we shake things up at the Loftus Versfeld in Pretoria?

It was another pleasant afternoon, without a breeze, the temperature in the sixties and a crowd of over seventy-five thousand people. Whatever the result, a record was bound to be broken, as no Lions squad had won the final test before, and South Africa had never won all four test matches. Nine out of ten people would have predicted victory for South Africa, without doubt. The Lions' forwards were dominant once again, and most of the first half was spent putting

Clive Rees and I close in on Clive Woodward at Twickenham in 1982. He proved himself a top coach when England won the World Cup in Australia in 2003.

immense pressure in the opponents' twenty-two. We fully deserved to be ahead by 7-3 thanks to a penalty kick from Ollie Campbell, and a try scored by prop Clive Williams. South Africa's response was a penalty kick by Naas Botha. After the forwards' great effort, reaching half-time with only a four-point advantage was disappointing, but in the second half, we, as backs, created movements that led to two tries – one for Andy Irvine and the other for John O'Driscoll. Some self-respect was restored at Pretoria with a fully deserved 17–13 win. Personally, I'm convinced of one thing; if we hadn't had so many injuries we would have completely hammered the buggers!

11

The Last Prince

It was great to feel the wheels of the aeroplane touching down on Heathrow's runway at the end of the Lions' tour. As we'd come to expect, reporters were waiting for us in the lobby at Heathrow, cameras and notebooks at the ready. One HTV reporter stuck a microphone under my nose and asked me what it was like to be back home. I answered by saying that I wasn't home yet . . . I wouldn't be home until I crossed the Loughor bridge, and I was really looking forward to having a pint of Buckley's beer. Following that conversation, I could have been accused of turning professional, because by the time I reached Kidwelly, there were a dozen bottles of Buckley's beer waiting for me – with compliments from one of the brewery directors!

Being at home also meant that I'd have to take on my new responsibilities as Llanelli captain, and I'd also decided that the club's demands would have priority over everything else during the season. So, after a break of three weeks, training began again with the coach, John Maclean. He had replaced Norman Gale as club coach, and I was pleased to see that John also encouraged open and creative play.

'Mr Don Hughes, it wasn't a late tackle. I got there as soon as I could!'

On the first night of training as I was driving in through the beautiful gates that lead to Stradey, I was astounded to see gigantic red letters on the side of the Clubhouse, declaring that we were at:

LLANELLI RUGBY FOOTBALL CLUB

I was so angry that I nearly drove my car into the wall. There was a full committee meeting that evening so I decided to do something about it there and then. I went to the committee room, knocked on the door, and waited. I couldn't go in as the door was locked, but the secretary, Ken Jones, opened it, and I asked if I could address the meeting as I had something important to say. My request to speak to the committee was granted, and I explained that I'd just seen the English-only sign on the club wall, and that I felt, considering our history and tradition, as well as the fact that we were located in a Welsh-speaking heartland, that the sign should be bilingual. The committee listened politely to what I had to say, and I was thanked for my contribution. I then joined John Maclean and the other players. And that was that.

But the following Wednesday, as I drove through the entrance, I saw the following words on the wall:

CLWB RYGBI LLANELLI RUGBY FOOTBALL CLUB

Fair play to the committee, they'd not only listened, but had acted too, within forty-eight hours. The scoreboard had been in Welsh since Carwyn's days, and all the announcements were made bilingually. Although these elements were just a public façade, I felt that they were very important, and I must say that encouraging the use of Welsh at Llanelli Rugby Club was a far easier battle than trying to get the WRU to adopt an official bilingual policy. Had Carwyn succeeded to get his foot through the door of the Union, I wonder whether he could have influenced the Union in the way that he did at Stradey. I'm afraid that he wouldn't have, as the WRU has always been a stubbornly conservative beast. It completely disregarded the Welsh language throughout the 1970s, although there have been signs over the past few seasons that it is, at last, beginning to see the light.

I wouldn't suggest for one minute that I had a successful first year as captain – even though we got to the Cup semi-final – because I had to master the art of people management, and learn that there are different ways of dealing with different players. Until then, I hadn't really considered the need to do that, perhaps as I'd been lucky enough to work with extremely good captains, who instinctively knew how to deal with players. But this was a slow and difficult process for me in the first season – learning to be sharp and firm with some, while giving others praise and encouragement.

In the early matches, I expected far too much of the team's younger players, and I'm afraid that I raised my voice more often than was necessary in those days. I remember having a long conversation with Carwyn about being captain, and he reminded me that it was easier to get the best out of someone through having a quiet chat rather than screaming all over the field. I took his advice to heart, and soon began to enjoy the responsibility of working on the principle that I should lead by example rather than preach. There were many very young players in the team that year – boys like Martin Gravelle and Kevin Thomas – and it was part of my responsibility to help them, and to give them advice whenever necessary. To this day, I certainly prefer being led to being leader, but by gaining more experience in that formidable job, leading others became easier for me. I had to change from being one of the foot-soldiers to being general, and that promotion was a heavy burden to carry in the early days. One of my responsibilities as captain was naming the vice-captain, and I chose a very promising wing-forward, who I believed would make his mark on the game within a year or two. David Pickering was a young man from Briton Ferry near Neath. He was full of enthusiasm and had been a very effective pack-leader during the season. He later gained widespread recognition as captain of his country, and I felt quite proud that I, perhaps, had contributed a little to the development of his leadership skills! My biggest disappointment in my first season as captain was losing against the All Blacks at Stradey, as I'd hoped that Llanelli would get into the record books by beating New Zealand on consecutive occasions. Although we failed to beat them, one infamous incident marred the match, when Graeme Higginson from New Zealand was sent off by the referee for kicking. This happened quite late in the second half, as we were playing towards the town end of the pitch, when Higginson, the visitors' second row, went into a ruck with his boot aiming for Charlie Thomas, our prop. Fortunately for Charlie, the kick was off target, and so Higginson ended up kicking Frank Oliver, one of his teammates, instead! Alan Hosie was there and saw the whole incident unfolding, and made a firm decision – blowing his whistle, raising his arm and pointing to the changing room, he shouted 'Off!' with no hesitation.

Phil Bennett ran towards him, and I wasn't far behind, and we only had one thing on our minds: preventing the referee from taking that step. I didn't want Higginson to be sent off the field because, up until then, it had been a hard game, but a clean one; and on top of that, hadn't he kicked one of his own players? As far as I knew, there wasn't a law that obliged referees to send players off for kicking one of their teammates! More importantly, perhaps, was the fact that the only thing that people would remember after the match was that a player had been sent off, and in a way, it could disgrace Llanelli, as well as the Welsh Rugby Union in its centenary year. All of this was rushing through my mind as I tried to persuade Mr Hosie to change his mind. At the same time, I was very aware of the fact that the referee has the final word, and that I shouldn't over-react – after all, arguments with referees tend to happen in football rather than rugby. After making my feelings clear, and Phil doing the same, I was relieved to see Mr Hosie blowing his whistle, bringing the match to an end there and then. He made a wise decision in my opinion, and avoided having to take the next step, even though there were a few minutes of play left. The incident became a sports quiz question for many years. In terms of the game itself, New Zealand deserved to win, and were the stronger team on the day.

I remember that match very clearly for another reason: before kick-off, I was in the changing room getting ready to talk to the players when Carwyn came in to give a few words of advice, and decided to stay during my speech. It was an emotional pep-talk to motivate the boys and to put them in the right frame of mind before stepping onto the field. A few days after the match, I was playing in Pontypridd when Gareth Price, head of the BBC's Welsh radio programmes at the time, came up to me and told me to listen to the radio on Friday night, as I would be appearing on one of the programmes. I couldn't, for the life of me, remember when I'd recorded the item. In fact, the item turned out to be my speech to the team before the match, and had been edited with more bleeps than was acceptable! I must admit that I felt very annoyed at the time, as Carwyn had recorded it all without telling me, and the BBC had broadcast the speech without asking my permission or giving any inkling that it would be on the radio. That evening at the Stradey Park Hotel, the captain was expected to make a speech, and I chose to do it through the medium of Welsh, and spoke about the similarities between the New Zealand Maori and the Welsh. To me, it was a totally natural thing to do, and although a few eyebrows were raised, I couldn't have done it any other way. A similar thing happened on the night I captained West Wales in the match against Australia, and at the end of that evening, the coach, Ieuan Evans, stood on his feet and applauded. He was the only one. I'll never forget his simple gesture, if only for making me feel that I wasn't entirely on my own after all. He showed his true colours that evening, and I appreciated it very much.

I remember another time when I travelled to Bangor as Carmarthenshire's captain. We had a wonderful reception at Bangor Rugby Club after the match, where the atmosphere was exceptionally warm and friendly, and I had to carry out my usual duties as captain. I explained my intention to speak in Welsh, and during the speech, three or four people walked out of the club. The only thing I can say is that it was their loss, as we had a fantastic social evening. We definitely need to sort out our own bigotry and intolerance in Wales before telling anyone else to put their own house in order.

In the Welsh Rugby Union's centenary year, I was on the bench against England and Scotland, with Steve Fenwick and David Richards featuring at centre. But in a move that surprised many people, I was recalled to the team against Ireland at the National Stadium, with Peter Morgan as my partner, and Gary Pearce (from Bridgend at that time) as outside-half. I kept my position against France in Paris too, and although we lost, David Richards scored a memorable try following his electrifying break.

During that season, I did something unforgivable in the eyes of the rugby fraternity, when I declined an invitation to play for the Barbarians at Northampton on a Wednesday afternoon. I refused because Llanelli had a game in Pontypridd that very evening, and my main responsibility was to lead my team whenever possible, especially as I'd decided to play as much as I could as captain. I never received an invitation to play for the Barbarians again! The reason for it could be that the Barbarians had heard me singing on the LP released by Sain, *Cewri'r Crysau Cochion*, to celebrate the centenary! That, on top of my habit of singing Dafydd Iwan songs in the changing rooms, was possibly more than they could handle! When the time came to elect a captain for 1981-2, I was elected unanimously for my second season. At least my co-players had faith in me.

The season was tainted by sadness, because on Boxing Day, during the traditional match against London Welsh, Bert Peel had a heart attack. Clive Norling was the referee on that Saturday afternoon and, during the game, I happened to notice people crowding together, and Bert Peel in his red tracksuit lying on the floor. I shouted at Mr Norling to stop the game, and ran over to

Bert, who was over on Stradey's popular bank. When I got there, he was sitting on the floor, fighting for breath, and like that character in the Geraint Griffiths song, 'Y *Ffeitar*', was obviously in a lot of pain. Two doctors came from somewhere, and asked for the stretcher. I walked beside him as he was being carried off the field, and he waved at the crowd before turning to face me. 'Everything's alright, Gravell bach, everything's alright, boy,' he said. Sadly, everything wasn't alright. He was rushed to Llanelli hospital, where he had yet another heart attack, which was more acute this time, and died later that afternoon. The rugby world lost an immensely likeable and good-natured character, I lost a very close friend, and a void was left in the Tumble and the Gwendraeth valley that would be impossible to fill; the same could be said for Glamorgan Cricket Club. The funeral held the following week was testament to the Tumble man's popularity – hundreds upon hundreds came to pay their last respects to him. A part of Llanelli Rugby Club was laid to rest that day, with Bert going to meet his Maker, true to his dying wish, wearing the club's red tracksuit.

Soon after the New Year, the touring Australian team arrived, and I was chosen as captain of the West Wales team to play against them at Stradey. This was the tour that demonstrated the Australians' new and exciting way of playing for the first time, with the Ella brothers artfully weaving their way through the defence.

The West Wales team was soundly defeated, and given a lesson in basic skills, which was a great benefit to the younger players. The game didn't do much to impress the selectors for the international season, and neither did the tactics I chose to beat Neath Athletic in the Cup.

'I totally disagreed with what you did this afternoon, Ray,' – Carwyn chastised me, in his own caring way.

'I thought that winning was the important thing, especially in a cup match,' was my defence.

'I agree,' said the master, 'but we should always win with flair – that's what's important.'

The selectors obviously agreed with the master's opinion about my performances, as Pat Daniels was chosen for the national team at the beginning of the season, but I was back to play the French at the Arms Park at the beginning of February.

The press were exceptionally kind about our victory, as well as my success in creating a try for Terry Holmes, with Robert Ackerman's help, during the last quarter of the game. JBG in the *Western Mail* firmly believed that I was much

1982 – my last season in a Welsh shirt. Terry Holmes scored a try and Gwyn Evans kicked six penalties. Carwyn would have approved of this pass, don't you think?

too slow to play centre for Wales ever again, but others disagreed – the Sunday papers were full of headlines such as, 'The Man Who Was Too Slow', and 'Slow-coach speeds through French', and 'Slow is too quick, *mon ami*'. It was heartening to read them, and our hopes were raised for the match at Twickenham. But we lost the game, and it's strange how the press – full of praise just a fortnight earlier – were baying for my blood, and the blood of other players too, after the match against England.

However, there was one match left, which was the game against Scotland at the National Stadium, on the same day that Ireland were striving to win the Grand Slam in Paris. Everything went wrong that day, and many hearts were broken. I remember praying, about six minutes from the end, for the referee to blow his whistle and bring an end to the whole nightmare. I'd never felt like that on a rugby field before, and consequently, I started to ask myself whether there was something wrong with my attitude. I knew that I wasn't the first choice for many selectors that season, and I decided, quite firmly, that I was going to end my international career that day, after twenty-three games for Wales and four tests in the Lions' jersey. I had no complaints, although being left out of the Welsh team was quite disappointing for me. I knew full well that everyone had to face this in the end, and apparently, I told some of the selectors on the evening of the match against Scotland that they wouldn't have the opportunity to leave me out again. Despite that, I decided to wait until the '82/83 season before making any announcements. And that's how it went. Although I started playing at Stradey with zeal and a fresh outlook, I took the step, and announced that I wouldn't play international rugby again. I'd been representing my country since 1975, but now I knew for certain that it was my ultimate decision. I've often considered what my response would have been had the selectors chosen me! Would they have selected me, I wonder.. ? I can definitely say that September and early October was a great period for me on the field. Perhaps it was because a load had been lifted off my shoulders. I wasn't elected Llanelli

Rutherford and Renwick stifle another attack as Wales are hammered by the Scots, and my international career draws to its close on March 20, 1982.

captain for the third time, with Phil May becoming captain for his first season, and he insisted that I became his vice-captain. I had the best beginning ever to a season – better than any of the previous twelve seasons. I'd already played four hundred games for the club, and was dreaming of reaching the five hundred mark.

The visitors at Stradey at the beginning of November 1982 were the Maoris from New Zealand, led by Paul Quinn, and to this day, I still remember the thoughts and emotions that were roused in that match. Would it be my last appearance against a visiting team? Certainly not, if it was down to me, and reporters were already predicting that I'd be a member of the Lions' squad that would travel to New Zealand in the summer of '83. I was revitalised, and seemed to be having a resurgence; we had an unforgettable 16-9 victory against the Maoris, in front of a crowd of sixteen thousand.

On Monday, January 10th, 1983, the telephone rang in my office in Llanelli, with Phil Bennett at the other end breaking the news of Carwyn James's tragic death in Amsterdam. I couldn't believe it. Totally unreasonably, perhaps, one feels that some people will never die, and to me, Carwyn was one of those people. On the one hand, Wales was much too small to lose such an immense talent; yet again, Wales was much too small to keep him to itself. Everyone wanted a piece of his genius, and it was difficult for him to say no to anyone. He'd often be in a quandary, trying to keep on top of his endless work and engagements. *The Guardian* demanded his time, and so did the BBC; players relied upon his help, and societies all over Wales were desperate to arrange an evening with him. The country that raised him suffocated him in the end.

Over the next few days, obituaries were published and tributes were paid, and many people who did nothing but criticize him when he was alive were now queuing up with their eulogies to him. Where the hell were those people when he was alive? Where were they indeed when Carwyn was eager to share his wealth of knowledge and experience? He had so much to give but, unfortunately, there's not only a north-south divide in our little country, but also a boundary between east and west, and although it might be a cliché to say that a prophet is never recognized in his own land, I also feel that Carwyn was recognized and respected by west Wales, but totally rejected by the east. If we had a Protestant Cathedral, it would have been completely jam-packed for his funeral. What chance did the little chapel in Cefneithin have to take in those who came to pay their last respects to a genius, a friend and a total expert in his field? I remember Gerald Davies saying on the weekend of the funeral that there was a deep feeling of guilt throughout Wales for not making the most of Carwyn Rees James's talent.

To me, Carwyn's secret was his ability to communicate with every player he was involved with, and to understand their way of thinking. He had that rare intellectual ability of being able to change a person's opinion in an argument, and could tune into the wavelength of the least capable players in order to get exactly the same effort out of them as the others. I never saw a player ignoring him. In conversation, his input was always constructive, and he always brought opposing factions together, without dismissing, hurting or dividing people. That afternoon, while I'd been given the honour of being a coffin bearer, the ultimate homage to Carwyn was taking place at Stradey. The Llanelli players had paid a tribute to Carwyn the previous week at St Helen's, but on the afternoon of the funeral, the game between Llanelli and Cardiff was the best tribute that he could have wished for, with his favourite team – and only team – displaying talent and skills that would have thrilled the master himself. That Saturday afternoon proved how blind and conservative the Welsh Rugby Union had been over the years. Carwyn had travelled extensively and had dazzled people all over the world with his talents, but those talents weren't given the recognition they deserved in his own country. Conventions, constitutions and order were placed above genius, vision and talent. It was too late to pay an empty tribute after his death. The establishment, the Welsh Rugby Union, believed that its own conventions were more important than the game itself. That same establishment's distrust of Welsh nationalists was further proof that the game and its institutions were deemed to be more important than language and tradition. That's the body that Carwyn tried to become a part of. He was snubbed. Carwyn never denied his heritage, and used every possible opportunity to express his opinion in his impeccably polite and gracious manner. There was now a big void to fill in Welsh-speaking Wales.

Cup semi-final against Bridgend at St Helen's. Selwyn Williams and I threaten from a scrum as Gerald Williams and Steve Penry-Ellis look to defend.

Without the stress of being captain, I could now enjoy every match, but I was fully aware of the fact that I wasn't getting any younger, and things started to go pear-shaped in the match against South Wales Police at Waterton Cross. Llanelli were well ahead, and I was facing Richard Donovan who'd had his first cap for Wales the previous year. When he got the ball, I charged towards him like a bull, in such a way that I could've ended up breaking my neck. I didn't do that, thankfully, but as I hit my shoulder against his thigh, I knew that I'd broken something, even though nothing came up on the X-ray at Llanelli hospital.

Monday morning, still in agony, I drove to Glangwili, where I saw Howard Davies, the specialist, who found that I'd split my shoulder in two – it came as a bit of a shock to him as it was the first example he'd seen in rugby. I was out of the Llanelli team for almost the whole season, and the following season, as I'd started appearing on television programmes, I was restricted to only ten games because of filming engagements, but was called upon to play against Australia in the '84/85 season, a game which Llanelli won.

By now, two new faces were coaching the club – two young men with whom I'd shared many experiences in my career, two talented players in their own right. The first, Gareth Jenkins, had captained the Wales youth team when I played, and was a top-class wing-forward, and his partner, Allan Lewis, who was a centre until a cruel injury prevented him from fulfilling his great potential.

At the beginning of 1985, when it had been snowing heavily, I had to travel to Llandovery for the Cup competition. I felt the old passion returning, and my enthusiasm growing. I managed to make two or three breaks, and was enjoying the match, until I jumped on a loose ball that had been kicked across the field. That very second, the hooker, David Fox, thundered towards me, and out of the

Another career beckons... In this instance interviewing ex-Llanelli and Wales scrum half, and former Llanelli chairman, Handel Greville.

corner of my eye, I saw his foot aiming for the ball, that was now behind me. I couldn't do anything except lift my arm to protect my head. If contact had been made, my head would have been kicked as far as Rhandir-mwyn. When I got to Glangwili hospital, where I was told that I'd broken my arm, the doctor explained in terrifying detail what would have happened to me had I not lifted my arm. After four hundred and eighty-five matches, the final whistle blew, when I was forced to look at myself, my future, and everyone around me. Back in November 1982, Carwyn wrote about me in *The Guardian*:

> Gravell is passionately Welsh. Llywelyn, the last real Prince of Wales, died in 1282, but spiritually Gravell belongs to his army.

Well, Carwyn bach, in that last match, I was halfway to Cilmeri to joining that army!

I would have enjoyed meeting Che Guevara. Red Ape Arising, the group responsible for the unofficial Scarlets website, saw the resemblance!

12

To the Battlefield

I didn't really think about my Welshness until my teens, when certain events made me question my identity and beliefs. Welsh was the language of my childhood, and Mynyddygarreg was a bastion of the Welsh language. Politically, my region was socialist, and at election time, I'd be very surprised if fewer than ninety-five percent of voters put their 'X' next to the Labour candidate. The village was deeply rooted in the Gwendraeth valley coal seam, and the miners' hardship under tyrannical pit owners had created a deep suspicion of capitalism. Not surprisingly, its inhabitants became staunch supporters of Mabon, Keir Hardie, Aneurin Bevan and Jim Griffiths. This was the background of my upbringing, and we never discussed nationalism at home, as it was the battle between pit proprietors and miners – between two social classes – that underpinned the politics of the area. My awareness of my Welsh identity was strengthened, as I've already mentioned, when I heard Dafydd Iwan singing his early songs on the television programme *Y Dydd*, and gradually, I absorbed some of his ideas, as I became more aware of Wales's political struggle to preserve its language and heritage. I didn't really consider the implications of my new-found beliefs, because I felt, as a teenager, that everyone thought the same way as I did, and that my response was totally natural.

The experience of having my first cap for the Wales youth team, and having to sing 'God Save the Queen' instead of '*Hen Wlad fy Nhadau*' on the field was distressing enough, but realising that I was the only one that seemed bothered about it was even more upsetting. Why didn't the other players feel that they were being disloyal to their Welsh roots? Was it a reflection of their background and education? Also, I don't remember having any history lessons based on Welsh history – it was all British history which focussed mainly on events in London. Having reached the top in rugby, I was put in the limelight, not from personal choice, but I decided early on in my career that I would make the most of every opportunity to get my views across. When I got to know Carwyn James, I gained a genius of a friend who was a great influence on my rugby playing and, even more importantly, a teacher who shaped and informed my Welsh patriotism. He spent many hours teaching me about some of our past heroes, as well as our most important literary figures. I got to know the poet Gwenallt through my friendship with Carwyn, and he opened my eyes by sharing his knowledge about events in recent Welsh history, such as the Penyberth incident and the development of Plaid Cymru. Very few rugby players can say that they learned so much about history, literature and politics on rugby trips. Unfortunately, Carwyn was a one-off person, and as a consequence, his influence was limited to a fortunate few who had the honour of spending time with him. If he'd succeeded in breaking through the prejudice of the Welsh Rugby Union, who knows how far his influence could have spread?

My contact with the Urdd Gobaith Cymru movement as a child was limited – my only involvement was paying my membership fee and

Complete with Mr Urdd sweatshirt, chatting with two of the Viet Gwent, Terry Cobner (left) and Graham Price.

attending meetings held in school. Over the years, I realized the importance of the movement to modern Wales, especially in terms of entertainment aimed at young people. It was at the Urdd camps in Llangrannog and Glan-llyn that the fledgling Welsh pop scene developed from the 1960s onwards, and the camps also gave many young people who were non-Welsh speakers the opportunity to use the language for the first time. We'd be a much poorer country without the activities that happen in these centres, and that is also true about the Urdd Eisteddfod. Where else in the world would you see tens of thousands of children practising for months to recite and sing and dance at their local 'eisteddfod gylch'?

Therefore, when I was asked to give a helping hand to the movement, I felt that it was an honour to do so, but when Wynne Melville Jones, an Urdd official at the time, suggested that I should record a song to launch the Mr Urdd campaign, I thought that he'd completely lost the plot. But he managed to persuade me over lunch in Llanelli that I should take the plunge. He took a cassette out of his pocket and said, 'There you go, the tune and lyrics are on the tape – learn them and we'll record in three weeks.' Even then, Wynne Mel displayed great powers of persuasion, which served him well in years to come with his successful PR company, Strata Matrix. He left me at the Stepney Hotel in Llanelli, with a tape of Geraint Davies's song in my hand, and his request ringing in my ears. I could do nothing but learn the song, and contact its composer to arrange one practice, the night befor the recording session.

I travelled to Aberystwyth, to Geraint and Siân's home, and after practising for hours that night, '*Y Fi a Mistar Urdd a'r Crysau Coch*' was more or less ready for the studio. Next morning, we travelled along the west coast towards North Wales and got to Waunfawr just in time for lunch at Marion and Dafydd Iwan's home. Do I know Dafydd Iwan? Too right I do! I've eaten his new potatoes! After lunch, we travelled to the old Sain studio in Llandwrog, where I was left on my own in the studio, wearing headphones. The music had been recorded beforehand, and I suddenly started to panic when it all rushed through my headphones, as it sounded quite different from the song on the cassette I'd been practising with. It was all a new and exciting experience for me, and I enjoyed it immensely, I must say – but more importantly, everyone seemed to be quite happy with the end result.

I had to wait for what seemed like ages for the release of the record. But at last, it was released and warmly received, and many copies were sold. Following the launch of the record and the Mr Urdd character, Geraint Davies had the idea of travelling around the country and staging concerts; to do that, we needed a lot of songs – so, we started preparing, using some songs by Dafydd Iwan and Tebot Piws (a well-known Welsh pop group), as well as some songs written especially for the tour by Geraint. Over the next few weeks, I travelled to village halls, schools and even a few pubs with Geraint and his guitar, with the aim of entertaining people and introducing the Mr Urdd character to them. I remember one visit to a Swansea valley school very well. It was full of young Welsh learners, and as usual, I was having a chat with them before 'performing'. I made the great mistake of asking which song they'd like to hear. The answer I had was, 'One of Shakin' Stevens's songs' – I was put in my place, there and then, by a little child!

The following months gave me a great opportunity to get to know Wales better, with the tour taking me from Treorchy to Tal-y-bont, and from Aberdare to Abergele. During the same period, I had the chance to sing with Dafydd Iwan at the Angel pub in Aberystwyth, to an audience comprising mainly of students. I was fully aware that Cymdeithas yr Iaith – the Welsh Language Society – was stronger in Aberystwyth than anywhere else at the time. During the course of the evening, I had to sing 'Y Fi a Mistar Urdd', with its chorus:

> *Roedd Llywelyn a Glyndŵr yn fois reit enwog,*
> *Ro'n nhw'n arwyr digon difyr yn eu ffyrdd;*
> *Ond o bawb ar draws y byd, fy newis i o hyd*
> *Fel arwr penna'r wlad yw Mr Urdd.*

(Llywelyn and Glyndŵr were quite famous fellows,
Admirable heroes, in their own way;
But out of everyone, across the world
Wales's biggest hero for me is Mr Urdd.)

When I came off the stage, I faced a barrage of extreme verbal abuse from one group in the audience, as I'd dared to joke about some of Wales's greatest heroes. Not only was I surprised, I was also very disappointed, I must admit, that those young people had reacted in such an unreasonable way to a song that was, to me, totally harmless. They obviously felt very strongly about it and saw everything in black and white, but I'm afraid that I left Aberystwyth that evening feeling very sad. However, I carried on promoting the Urdd whenever I had the opportunity to do so.

Phil Bennett, Keith Williams and I were never sure whether we should curtsy or not.

My singing often drew comments in the changing room, and the usual remark would be 'Grav and his bloody Welsh songs again!' But if that was the usual reaction, at least one player wanted to hear more singing – Terry Holmes would often say to me, 'Sing "Caa-low", Grav, sing "Caa-low",' and I'd have to go through '*Carlo*' once again. In the end, I gave him a copy of Dafydd Iwan's LP, and Terry still sings that chorus, with his 'Kerdiff' accent bringing a bit of an edge to '*Caa-low'n whare polo*.' In 1979 I was asked to record another song for an LP that would be released to celebrate the centenary of the Welsh Rugby Union, and once again, Geraint Davies started composing lyrics and a melody for '*Gêm y Bêl*'. The record sold very well, and I remember taking part in a ceremony to present the record to Graham Mourie, the New Zealand captain.

My involvement with Plaid Cymru was a bit of a talking point in rugby circles as well over the years, but I can't for the life of me see why, as it was totally unrelated to my rugby playing. I remember going to a training session at the Arms Park after recording a party political broadcast – the footballer John Mahoney did the English version while I recorded the Welsh one – and I took a pile of Plaid pamphlets with me. When I got back to the changing room after training, the pamphlets had been scattered all over the room, and some Union officials made a few snide comments about what I was doing. As I've already mentioned, the Union doesn't believe in open displays of Welsh patriotism, but I'm very proud of what I did.

Soon after losing my place for the second time in the Welsh team, I agreed to attend a Plaid Cymru evening in Pumsaint, where the special guests were Gwynfor Evans, who had just lost an election in Carmarthen, Dafydd Iwan who'd just lost his seat on Gwynedd Council, and me. I got quite a few laughs when I said that it was a special evening, as the village had the pleasure of having three failures as special guests. Yet, despite those recent disappointments, there was a feeling of unity that evening – a sense of coming together to protect our treasured language, traditions and culture.

In 1981, I was given the greatest honour that any Welshman could have, when I received a letter inviting me to become a member of the Gorsedd of Bards, and to attend the inauguration ceremony at the Machynlleth National Eisteddfod. To me, an honour such as the MBE and OBE seemed irrelevant and inappropriate, but this was different, and although I'd seen other players such as Gareth Edwards and Gerald Davies becoming Gorsedd members, I didn't dream for one second that the same honour would be bestowed on me. It was one of

The Crowning ceremony at the National Eisteddfod in Llanelli, 2000.

the highlights of my life – whatever people say about the Gorsedd and its pomp and ceremony, it's an important institution to honour the people of this nation. I didn't have the talent to make a cultural or literary contribution to Welsh life; the only gift I had was my ability to play rugby and my Welshness. I didn't have a university degree or the ability to take the Gorsedd examinations, so the invitation to join meant more to me than words could ever express.

If I could be anyone other than myself, I would, without doubt, like to be a poet. I'd happily trade in every Welsh cap and Lions shirt, just to have the thrill of standing up in the Eisteddfod pavillion, under the spotlight, for the crowning or chairing ceremony. I experienced that thrill watching the young Siôn Eirian receiving the poet's crown, and the experience was even more thrilling at the Rhyl Eisteddfod when Robat Powel rose, and was wildly applauded by the crowd. To me, that was one of the most important events at the Eisteddfod. After all, Robat had learnt Welsh as a second language, and had not only mastered the language, but also the art of *cynghanedd* (strict-metre verse) to such an extent that he won Wales's most prestigious poetry prize. If only I had his talent!

The inauguration ceremony in Machynlleth was a day that I'll always treasure, and perhaps the fact that Jâms Niclas, a neighbour from Kidwelly, was the Archdruid, made it even more personal for me. I had the very pleasant company of Arthur Rowlands, the policeman and broadcaster who was blinded in a shooting incident, and from that day onwards, we became good friends. Nothing gives Arthur more pleasure than going to an international match at the National Stadium, with a companion to describe the match for him, as he breathes in the atmosphere, with a big smile on his face. On the morning of the ceremony, it rained for the first time that week, which meant that everything had to happen in the local secondary school; so, I didn't have the experience of a ceremony inside the Gorsedd stone circle. Fair play, Gerald Davies came to the meeting too, to support me on my big day.

I had to smile in the changing room that morning, with so many men wearing thermals underneath their green, blue and white gowns – quite a different experience to rugby changing rooms! But I certainly learned my lesson that day, because I wore the green gown over my clothes, and by the afternoon on the pavillion stage, I was sweating buckets as I watched the ceremony from a new and completely different angle. I will treasure that wonderful Thursday forever; it's a bigger honour than becoming a Sir or a Lord could ever be. I was bestowed an honour by my own countrymen, which can never be taken away from me. Of course, it's possible that the Gorsedd is nothing but a figment of Iolo Morganwg's florid imagination, but to me, the pageant and ceremony has an important place in Wales today.

A few days before the Eisteddfod, I received a letter from Angharad Tomos of Cymdeithas yr Iaith, asking whether I had a gift to donate to an auction to raise money for the Society during the Eisteddfod. Angharad's letter created quite an impression – it was written on red paper! So, I took one of my most valuable rugby shirts to the auction at the Lampeter Eisteddfod – the Llanelli shirt from the legendary match against New Zealand in 1972 – and I realized, as I presented the shirt to her, that Angharad knew very little indeed about rugby. But I also realized how dedicated she was to her work, and how important the Society's campaign was to her. Perhaps some of her enthusiasm rubbed off on me, as I became more aware of the struggle to preserve the Welsh language and culture after seeing her willingness to give up her freedom for the cause. Although the Llanelli shirt didn't mean a lot to Angharad, I'm glad to say that at least one person in the auction was willing to pay over one hundred pounds for it. I later had a chance to visit Angharad at home in Llanwnda near Caernarfon, where I received a very warm welcome from her parents. Their home was unique as it wasn't monopolised by a television set – they didn't have one – and her parents, despite suffering abuse from local people, were very supportive of their daughter's stance. Thank God for strong people like that, I say.

Gradually, through the influence of many people I've already mentioned, I started to learn more about the Welsh-language media, and after being interviewed many times on the radio and television, I started to look for a career in that direction, even though I felt my chances were slim in those early days. One thing is certain: the fact that I was a Welsh speaker was hugely important from the word go, especially as my very first interview at the beginning of my career had been on Radio Cymru, one Saturday back in the early 1970s. That interview caused me some trouble during my time as an international player, as the Welsh Rugby Union banned every player from giving interviews before a match, a rule that, in my mind, impeded personal freedom under the rules of the amateur game. Why shouldn't a player have the freedom to express an opinion? The Welsh Rugby Union insisted on having complete control over players – their bodies and minds – and it angered me to see this suppression going on.

I'm afraid that I completely broke that rule before one match at the Arms Park. We'd reached the changing room early, and as usual, the other team had gone onto the pitch about an hour before kick-off, before the crowd had started to enter, and as we made our way through the tunnel towards the field, we had to go past the little radio studio. Inside, I could see Huw Llywelyn Davies, microphone in hand, and John Evans. The microphone has always been like a magnet to me, so I went over for a chat – and the interview ended up being broadcast as part of the big match build-up. One of the selectors still happened to be in his hotel, and after hearing the interview, lodged an official complaint to the Union that two BBC reporters had broken the rule. As a consequence, Huw and John were banned from doing interviews for the rest of the season. Both of them had a lot of publicity in the press after that, and so if all publicity is good publicity, perhaps I gave their careers a boost!

Yes, I gave many interviews over the years, both officially and unofficially, but in 1977, I had my big chance – nearly! The BBC were filming *Grand Slam* and, of course, that film included footage of the France v Wales game in Paris.

Wales win the game in the film – though no one explained that to the French – and I was meant to appear in one scene, celebrating the victory. But I ended up having a shoulder injury which meant that I couldn't play in the match. In the end, they had to change the script, and my opportunity, like the ball that afternoon, didn't make it through the posts.

Soon afterwards, however, I was invited to appear in a short scene in *Pobol y Cwm*, because John Hefin, the producer, had heard that I liked to impersonate Caleb, the likeable mole on the popular Welsh programme for children, *Miri Mawr*. To this day, many people still believe that I really was Caleb. That didn't go down very well with Dafydd Hywel, the actor in the

Elin and John Hefin – two of our dearest friends – at Borth beach.

Dafydd Hywel (on the right) and Gladys.

mole suit! I was introduced to the real Caleb at Stradey by Carwyn James, when Dafydd Hywel was playing for Clwb Rygbi Cymry Caerdydd against Llanelli Athletic, at a time when many Stradey players such as Hefin Jenkins and Selwyn Williams were great fans of Caleb and *Miri Mawr*. Caleb's catchphrase – '*Grynda 'ma, Byti boy,*' – became a popular greeting at Stradey! Because of this, I found myself at the BBC studios, on the set of *Pobol y Cwm*. In my scene, I pop into the Deri Arms for a packet of cigarettes, and the locals accuse me of being Caleb. I only had about six lines, but it was enough to give me a taste of

Appearing in *Pobol y Cwm* with Lisabeth Miles (1975).

drama and performing. It was good fun, and I can't have been too bad as I was invited back, two years later, to visit the Deri Arms again. Soon afterwards, I appeared as a beauty-contest judge in the comedy series, *Glas y Dorlan*.

Each one of those opportunities fuelled my desire to get more media work. In each one of those appearances, I was Ray Gravell the rugby player, and I must admit that I longed for a chance to hide behind another character once in a while, to have a go at acting! The opportunity came from a totally unexpected source, with a phone call from Gwynne D. Evans, the playwright from Cross Hands, asking me to audition for a part in his play *Pen y Daith*, which was written to celebrate the four hundredth anniversary of Carmarthen Grammar School – The Gram. I was cast, and began rehearsing my role in the play, which was staged for two nights in Carmarthen, with experienced actors such as Ernest Evans, Haydn Edwards, Buddug Williams and Marian Fenner – actors who later became household names on *Pobol y Cwm*, and Glyndwr Walker, who taught me at the Gram. My next opportunity came at the beginning of the 1980s, with a request from Peter Elias Jones, Ronw Protheroe and Paul Jones for me to go to the HTV headquarters in Cardiff to audition for a programme that was being prepared, for which they wanted four presenters. I did the audition with little confidence, and heard the familiar words at the end, 'You'll hear from us.' To my surprise, I did hear from them, and was invited to co-present the programme *Teulu Ffôn*, a pioneering series for Welsh television, as it would be broadcast live, with many different events, competitions as well as sketches, in which I'd act. This weekly programme was a fantastic opportunity to establish a career for myself, and I now knew the direction I wanted to aim for.

I'll never forget one evening, when I was responsible for the poets' corner, with Dic Jones on one side and the legendary prankster, Dewi 'Pws' Morris on the other. For some reason, I didn't see the stage manager's sign, indicating that there was only half a minute left; I could only see his arms flailing all over the place, and Dewi Pws responding to the waving with a Hitler salute. I don't know how we

Two of the main men on S4C's Y Clwb
Rygbi – Huw Llywelyn Davies (left) and
Brynmor Williams.

managed to film that night. Those experiences forced me to become more disciplined, as I had to learn the script in the morning, ready to film the programme in the evening. It was a bit of a problem at the beginning, until I became used to it. When the series ended, I thought that my career as a presenter-actor was over, but I was offered a small part in Siôn Eirian's first television series, *Bowen a'i Bartner*, and this time, I played a completely different character from Ray Gravell.

With the establishment of S4C, I also had a chance to be a summarizer with Huw Llywelyn Davies at international matches. I clearly remember the first match to be broadcast on the channel with Welsh commentary. Wales were playing against England at the Arms Park in Cardiff in 1983, and the producer, Geraint Wyn Davies, had asked me to be at the field about an hour before the game. I did as I was told. At that time, the south stand hadn't been completed, so, I had to walk all around the pitch to reach the commentators' booth. I spent some time signing programmes for children who were already at the ground, and when I was almost by the booth, I saw David Coleman knocking on the window, calling me into a room, where he was talking to Billy Beaumont. They asked me to have a few words with them for *Grandstand*. I agreed, but unfortunately, we had to wait for a horse race to finish before the interview could commence. In the meantime, in S4C's booth, Huw Llywelyn Davies, the producer, and Onllwyn Brace, Head of Sports Programmes for BBC Wales, were anxiously waiting for me, as I was late for the broadcast. Suddenly, they happened to look at the TV monitor in front of them, and saw their summarizer being interviewed on BBC1. It was a bit of a shock, and Onllwyn was furious – apparently, he shouted, 'What the hell is he doing there when he's meant to be here?' When I arrived, with only a few minutes to go, he only calmed down when I explained that I'd given a lot of publicity on *Grandstand* to the historic broadcast on S4C.

Carwyn supported me throughout my career, and in a way, was partly responsible for guiding me towards the media, by bringing me into discussions about rugby on radio programmes. He was the master of post-match analysis, and since his death, no one has come close to stepping into his shoes. But it was time for me to change direction. There were rumours that HTV wanted me to present programmes for S4C. I'd presented many programmes for Radio Cymru from the Swansea studio, but I had no concrete plans for the future.

Then, one morning in June, I got back to my office in Llanelli, and Susanne, my secretary, told me that Onllwyn Brace from the BBC had phoned, and that he would ring back in ten minutes. The phone call came, and Onllwyn's voice explained that the BBC wanted to offer me a two-year contract, beginning in September '85, and that the contract would mean giving up playing for Llanelli, as my work would include commentating on games every Saturday afternoon, as well as presenting a few other programmes on Radio Cymru. My reaction was a bit mixed, as I was only fifteen games away from the five hundred mark. But to be fair, I had to think of the future – playing my five hundredth game wouldn't pay the mortgage. So, I decided to take the step, which meant leaving Stradey behind. A new chapter was beginning.

13

Number 13

Beginning a new career brought another career to an end, in a way – a career that saw me wearing the number thirteen shirt for sixteen years, as a member of Llanelli Rugby Club. I never thought about leaving the club – even though I was once invited to join the capital city's team – which would have meant crossing Loughor bridge far too often for my liking. An invitation also came to travel even further, to play professionally in the north of England, but I must be honest and say that even twenty-five thousand pounds couldn't tempt me to leave my own patch – I'd rather have played for Swansea!

Because of the game, I had more opportunities than most people to travel the world, to make friends in all four corners, and to be in the public eye for a long time. Looking back, it's far easier to remember the highlights rather than the disappointments. If I'd started writing this a few years ago, it's possible that I would have been more negative and critical, and would have felt more bitterness towards certain people and events. I'm relieved that I didn't do that. I have no reason to be discontented, because I got so much out of the game, and it's fair to say that rugby also gave me a second career.

The most memorable events have already been chronicled in detail, but I'm sure that I'll always look back to October 1972, and hear Carwyn James's

Ready for a change of scene.

words in my ears, 'Grav, today's a big day for you. Today you'll get the chance to show that you're going to play for Wales.' Although the whole team deserved credit for the result, Carwyn was the architect of it all. He planned our victory carefully.

But my memories are also tinged with sadness. Losing my father at such a young and impressionable age left a void that was impossible to fill. As I grew older, the void turned into a massive gulf. I often felt a deep longing for someone to lean on, to turn to for advice, but I could only see my father's face, in constant pain. The passage of time has numbed the ache, but it will never disappear.

I'm sure that some events will remind me of the time I lost my place in the Wales team – I remember feeling terribly hurt at the time – but it did prick my inflated ego, and made me realize that there were other good players around. Another sad turn of events was the fact that my marriage to Aurona disintegrated, and I had to face the fact that my selfishness was to blame. I was captivated by crowds and audiences, and used to run back to my old village when the going got tough, which was far easier than fighting to save our relationship when it broke down. Although I remember many happy times, I can't forget my darkest days.

Since leaving Stradey as a player, and turning to broadcasting, I've been compelled to look at rugby in a different way. Not in a more serious way, as I still feel that it's a game to be enjoyed. Far too many supporters, administrators and reporters take it extremely seriously, which means that the main purpose of the game is lost on them, which is the pure pleasure that it gives players and supporters, on the field as well as in social occasions related to the game.

After ending my international career, and being invited to commentate on the most important games, the first season was very difficult for me, as I often felt that I wanted to be out on the pitch. As a consequence, being unbiased was painfully difficult at times. Occasionally, I'd have to be critical, and in doing that, I was very aware of the fact that I could be accused of being envious or malicious, especially as I was, at the time, still playing for Llanelli. I'm sure that I felt, more than once, that I could do just as well, if not better, than some of the players on the field, but I'd taken my decision and had to stick to it.

At the beginning, expressing my opinion on a match was difficult, but by now I love commentating on every match, whatever its standard, because every game has something to offer. For example, commentating on the final round of the Tovali Cup at Stradey between Tumble and Carmarthen Athletic, and at the National Stadium in the Schweppes Cup final between great teams like Cardiff and Newport – although that game turned into the best advert that rugby could ever wish for. By now, I look at every game objectively, even when I'm commentating at Stradey, although a few colleagues would beg to differ! This painful transition is experienced by every ex-player, as many become coaches or referees, or even committee members and administrators. After all, no one can change the habits of sixteen seasons overnight!

There's nothing easier than sitting comfortably in the stand, being extremely critical of playing standards. A player on the rugby stage has a split second to make a decision, and if he hesitates, his choices all disappear. It's so easy for commentators to observe everything from above, and to see it all like a game of chess! It's much harder for the player on the field to see it that way, and I often feel quite annoyed with some commentators for being overly critical of some players for taking a wrong decision. Harsh criticism can impede a young player's development; very often, it's not constructive criticism, and if I were guilty of doing that, I'd have no right to be in this job. With developments in the media and television, mistakes in rugby games are thoroughly scrutinized, with incidents being replayed time and time again, whether they're examples of dirty play, a thrilling try, or a mistake by the referee. Although this can add to the viewer's pleasure, it puts more pressure on those who are involved in the game – sometimes for the best, but often not.

The number thirteen on my back brought me luck in my career. I'll treasure each and every one of those memories – the good and the bad – with gratitude for all the opportunities I had.

Part 2

To the Mountain
1987–2007

1

'There's no place like home'

Paradise

Camelot, Paradise, Heaven – or, in other words, Mynyddygarreg. Every morning as I look out from the bathroom window I never fail to marvel at the view that greets me, it's pure magic. Within a stone's throw of my home, Brynhyfryd, stands Horeb Chapel – the original building was built in 1741 using red brick which was produced locally, and its main claim to fame was that one of the founding meetings of the Methodist Revival took place in the building.

I myself owe the chapel a debt of gratitude. Here as a young lad I learned not only a range of Bible stories but also the core values and moral standards which help to mould an individual into a responsible human being.

It is this tradition of home, chapel and community that has produced such great Welshmen and women of the past and it is hoped that the tradition will continue for present and future generations. Mari and the girls still attend Horeb on a regular basis and are stalwarts of the Sunday school – something of which I am extremely proud, having enjoyed many a happy hour there myself (I still go occasionally but not as often as the girls). It was here at Mynyddygarreg that I started my life's journey and I cannot think of anywhere else where I would choose to end that journey.

An item on *Wedi 3* S4C (August 16, 2005)

I Grew Up on That Mountain

(*Ray was interviewed by Max Boyce on BBC Radio Wales's* The Final Curtain, *and asked where, when the time came, he would choose to spend his last day*).

No doubt in my mind at all. I was born in Kidwelly, my mother was from the town and my father was from Mynyddygarreg, a little village a mile-and-a-half up the road. I'm fifty-one years of age, and it's taken me forty odd years to realise the magic of Mynyddygarreg. There are views of Caldey Island, the Gower Peninsula including Worm's Head, the rolling hills of Dyfed, the lights of Carmarthen at night, the Gwendraeth fach.

Can you see Swansea from there?!

I most certainly can't see Swansea from here, although my grandmother was a Mumbles lady. The Irish poet Jonathan Swift or Dean Swift once wrote,

> I've often wish'd that I had clear,
> For life, six hundred pounds a year;
> A handsome house to lodge a friend;
> A river at my garden's end;
> A terrace walk, and half a rood
> Of land set out to plant a wood.

I've got it! I'd like more than £600 mind! I grew up on that mountain in Mynyddygarreg and it means so much to me

Ray for Ever!

I was secretly very pleased and proud when Carmarthenshire County Council offered to name our street 'Heol Ray Gravell'. The day for erecting the sign duly arrived and there was quite a stir in the village when the council workers finally finished the job.

I hadn't said anything to the girls, Manon and Gwenan, so they had quite a shock when they arrived home from school to see the new sign standing proudly at the end of the road. It was Manon who spoke first – 'Dad, "Heol Ray Gravell". Does that mean you're going to live for ever?' It was a question which shook me to the core – but it means that the name will live on even when the old boy is long gone.

Manon and Gwenan are chuffed with the sign.

A ratio of 3:1

It was love at first sight. The moment I set eyes on Mari I knew that there was something really special about her and when she admitted that she felt the same way about me – that was it! A marriage made in heaven.

The arrival of the girls only served to cement our relationship and now we are a close family unit. To be perfectly honest, I cannot imagine life without them – one man and his three girls! Mind you, when decisions have to be made the result is always three to one – no, make that four to one, as the cat always takes sides with the girls!

Mari, Manon and Gwenan.

August 2nd, 1991: Mari and I over the moon on our wedding day.

'Gas and Air'

(Transcribed and translated from Beti a'i Phobol, *a BBC Radio Cymru interview with Beti George.)*

Ray: Mari and I were married in August 1991, shortly after I first appeared on your programme, Beti. I suppose you could say that you played your part in matters, but without doubt, the highlight of our married life has been the birth of the girls, Manon and Gwenan. I was there on both occasions, you know, a miracle indeed – and I was a witness to it all.

Beti: Do you think having you present helped Mari?

Ray: Not at all! Of course, during the pregnancy, I'd attended the relevant classes, watched the video presentations, and joined in when Mari practised her deep breathing techniques, but . . .

Beti: Please don't tell me you fainted!

Ray: No, not quite but it was an incredible experience. I've not said this publicly before but it was the most amazing thing that has ever happened to me – being present at the birth of Manon first and then Gwenan. The two events were completely different, but each time I'd hold Mari's hand, breathe deeply when she did, feel the pains in my belly and take big gulps of the gas and air! When it was all over I was the one jumping up and down with tears of joy rolling down my cheeks.

Beti: How much help were you to Mari after the birth? Did you bath the girls, and change their nappies for example?

Ray: No, I have small hands but big feet. Yes, I did help out and I think it's important that fathers do their fair share – but the mother will always be the *numero uno*.

Beti: So any future sons-in-law will have to be pretty special if they are to be good enough for your girls!

Ray: Well, put it this way. If either of them brings a rugby player home to Mynyddygarreg, the first thing I'd do is castrate him!

Pinky

During my lifetime I have been very fortunate in that I have made hundreds of friends from all over the world – but some are more special than others. One of these is Pinky – Adrian Howells who was born and brought up in Carmarthen. We attended the Gram in the town at the same time and became close following the deaths of our respective fathers.

For me, the weeks following my dad's suicide were especially difficult, and the thought of returning to school filled me with dread. What would people say? What did they think? In fact, the whole scenario was a living nightmare. As it turned out of course, the teachers and my fellow pupils were very understanding and everyone was incredibly kind to me. As time passed, I began to settle back to some semblance of normality.

When Pinky returned to school following the passing of his own father, I was the first person he met at the school gates and because of my own experience I could understand what he was going through. From that moment, a special bond developed between us and it is a bond that has remained to this day.

During my last year at Queen Elizabeth Grammar School, Carmarthen, we both played in the senior rugby team. Impossible as it seems, Pinky played on the wing (anyone who knows him will confirm that Pinky today more resembles Billy Bunter than Gerald Davies). With Phil Thomas captaining the side, we had a very successful year defeating Llanelli, Neath, Llandeilo, Amman Valley and Maesydderwen schools.

Our success led to an invitation to play two games against Wallasey and Birkenhead schools. At that time, Birkenhead was a prestigious public school whose headmaster, John Gwilliam, was an iconic Welsh international back-row forward who had captained Wales during their Grand Slam successes in 1950 and 1952. The game was played on a Friday afternoon and I can remember giving a rendition of '*Calon Lân*' before leaving the changing rooms. For us, the

Carmarthen boys, this was no less than an international played on foreign soil and Welsh pride was at stake. As we took the field we were confident of a win and so were suitably humbled when the final score read Birkenhead 25 Carmarthen 0.

At the post-match dinner I was given the honour of being seated next to John Gwilliam. During our conversation I learned that he had played a couple of games for the Scarlets – his wife being a native of Llanelli. I believe he now lives in Moelfre, Anglesey, and has become a fluent Welsh speaker. Those school years were some of the best of my life and as I look back on them I am grateful for the part they played in developing my character and making me the person I am today.

Bosom pal – Adrian Howells (Pinky).

Pinky and I lost touch after we left school – he went on to learn his craft as a journalist, initially with the *Western Mail* and the *South Wales Evening Post* before becoming a producer of *Heno* and *Wedi 7* with Tinopolis on S4C. In the meantime I concentrated my energies on my rugby career.

Years later we met up again and resumed our friendship as if we had never been parted. What's so special about Pinky? Well, for a start he is someone you can rely on totally – kind, has a sense of humour, modest and utterly discreet. To be perfectly honest, at times I was a bit of a pain in the neck to Adrian. Sometimes, I would ring him two or three times a day with a query or for confirmation on a particular point and, as only true friends can say to each other, he'd answer the phone with the words, 'Oh no! What do you want now Grav?'

Good Friends, One and All

(From the left): Robert, Les and Raymond Williams from Kidwelly.

The Mynyddygarreg RFC Faithful: (from the left) Fred, Pam and Wyn Smyth.

The man that persuaded Carmarthenshire County Council to name the road – John 'Tremendous'.

A friend from primary-school days – Mike 'Bach'.

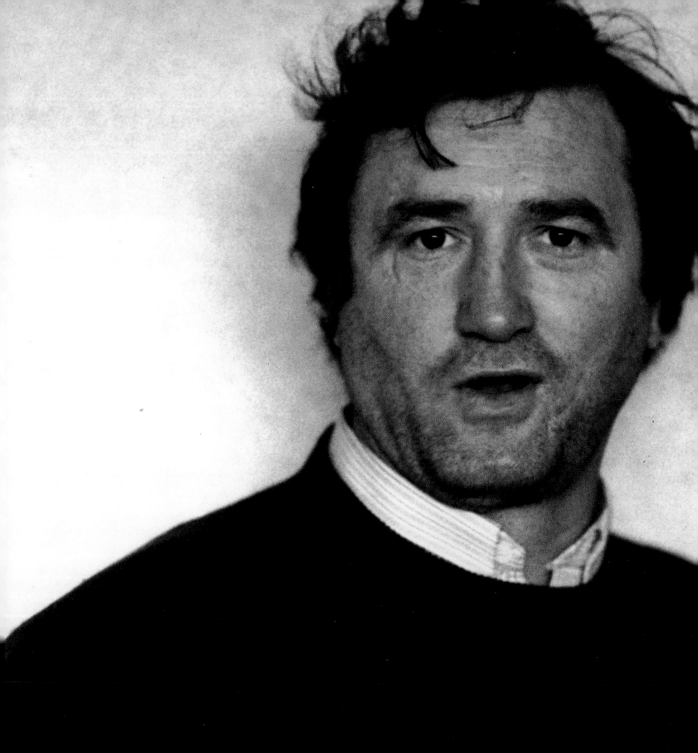

2

Stage and Screen

Tackling Lawrence of Arabia

(Ray had been given a small part in the film Rebecca's Daughters *directed by Karl Francis, and starring Peter O'Toole, Keith Allen and Joely Richardson)*

To say I was nervous was a bit of an understatement. I had even thought of taking a beta blocker before leaving home! On the drive from Mynyddygarreg to Brecon, all I could think of were the stars I would be meeting on the set that day. They were all household names, all superstars . . . and me!

I had been told to report to the make-up trailer by half past seven in the morning because it would take around two hours to get me ready for the first take. I would be playing the role of Jonah, one of Rebecca's daughters during the night-time raids, and as such would be dressed as they were in the nineteenth century, and as if this wasn't enough I had to have my face blackened as well.

Now let me tell you . . . before any rugby match, mine was the loudest voice in the changing room seeking reassurances from my team mates, questioning tactics and in fact doing anything to settle my nerves. Here, in the heart of the Brecon Beacons sitting in my chair as quiet as a mouse, I was patiently waiting for the make-up artist to start work on my transformation.

I flicked through the script, trying to pretend that I hadn't noticed who was sitting in the chair some six feet away from me. It was none other than Lawrence himself, the great Irish actor Peter O'Toole. He was having his face applied by one of the best make-up artists in the business, Marina Monias who was used to dealing with most of the big Hollywood stars. For her, this was just another day at the office. It was Marina who got the conversation going . . .

Marina: Peter, this is Ray.

Peter: *(Looking directly at the mirror in front of him)*: How are you?

Ray: Fine, thank you Mr O'Toole!

Marina: He's played a bit of rugby you know. In fact, he's quite friendly with Richard (Harris) and Terry (Dr Terry James).

        (Upon hearing this, the great man casually looked across. However, the nineteenth-century clothing meant that not even the good folk of Mynyddygarreg would have recognized me).

Peter: You've played rugby have you? Who did you play for?

Ray: I played 485 games for Llanelli during the 1970s and early 1980s.

Peter: That's a lot. Did you play against JPR?

Ray: Mr. O'Toole, I am honoured and privileged to have played with, and against, JPR, Gareth and Gerald.

Peter: *(By now the world-renowned star of the silver screen was clearly agitated)*: Which other teams did you play for?

Ray: I represented Wales, the Barbarians, and the British Lions as a centre threequarter . . . without forgetting Carmarthenshire!

Peter: You played for Wales! Who was the finest centre you played against?

Ray: That has to be the Ulsterman, Michael Gibson. A true great!

Peter: (*By now O'Toole was on his feet, scattering Marina's make-up bottles and staring at me with some intent*): You f***ing played against Mike Gibson! You're not that man mountain, Ray Gravell?

Ray: Well, yes I am!

Peter: Well, f***ing hell! You wait till I get back to London and tell them I'm making a film with Ray Gravell!

DH, Jack Walters and me on the set of *Rebecca's Daughters*.

During the two weeks we were on set, Peter O'Toole spent every spare moment with Dafydd Hywel, Huw Ceredig and yours truly. He was a rugby fanatic and wanted to know everything about what went on behind the scenes, what happened when we were on tour and any little titbits of scandal that I might have known. He was quite a character!

Of course, as the star of the film he had his own private trailer but he didn't spend much time in it. If anyone was looking for him, they would come to us in the extras tent because that's where he chose to spend his time.

The press were always hanging around looking for a story or a photo opportunity and he answered every request in the same way, 'Yes, I'll let you take a picture as long as Ray's in it!' After a while I became really embarrassed but one afternoon one photographer was heard to say to me, 'Get out of the way. We just want O'Toole.' The film star went bonkers. 'F*** ***! The shoot's over. Get out and don't come back,' he shouted.

I had several film offers after that, all minor roles of course. But I couldn't refuse opportunities of working with people like Jeremy Irons, Juliette Binoche and Ralph Fiennes.

Catherine Zeta Jones; almost as pretty as Mari.
Me: 'Catherine, if we come to live out here in LA – do I need to change my accent?'
Catherine: 'Ray – don't ever change'

De Niro or DH?

If someone decides one day to make a film about the life and times of Ray Gravell, there's only one person who can play the lead role and no, my friend (Dafydd Hywel), much as I love you, this time it won't be you – it has to be Robert de Niro.

There won't be a screen test or an audition, he already has the part! Should the director worry that de Niro's rugby skills aren't quite up to the mark, then I'm sure that modern technology will make him appear as a Gravell look-a-like. 'But he doesn't speak Welsh!' I hear you say. Well, back in the 1970s they successfully voiced a Welsh-language version of the cowboy film *Shane* with Alan Ladd made to sound as if he'd just completed an intense Welsh course at University College Wales, Lampeter. Friends, it won't prove a problem for the great de Niro.

Like most thespians I am superstitious and so before each take I like to hear the director shouting 'Action'. Then when I've done my bit and the day's filming is at an end I patiently wait for the technical crew to pose the question, 'Is that a wrap, director?' Yes, de Niro and I have a lot in common!

The panto *Zandor*

Angharad Roberts's costume fits like a glove!

Punk.

Buffalo Bill.

I would have loved to have played outside this pair – Scarlets, Wales and Lions halfbacks, Dwayne Peel and Stephen Jones.

3

West is Best

Aussie! Aussie! Aussie!

(Ray re-lives one of the truly great days in the history of Llanelli Rugby Football Club when the Scarlets defeated world champions Australia 13-9 at Stradey Park on November 14th, 1992. The chapter appeared in the book, Stradey Stories*)*

This is quite a statement. Some of you might well disagree. The 1992/93 season was a sensational one for Llanelli RFC – they claimed the Welsh Cup . . . again! They also won the league title and beat the world champions, Australia, in a thrilling contest at Stradey Park. Former players tend to romanticize about the past and I suppose I could recall great victories in the 1970s and especially the 1972/73 game when we defeated the All Blacks. I'm not going to do that. I saw the vast majority of the Llanelli matches during the '92/93 season, either in my role as S4C pundit or accompanying Mari to the front row of the grandstand where both of us supported enthusiastically. The players were outstanding, the style adopted bringing supporters to their feet in admiration, thanks to the positive attitude of the coaches who provided the players with a licence to thrill.

At the beginning of the 1990s, Gareth Jenkins and Allan Lewis were arguably the best coaches in Wales, if not in Britain. Their role model and mentor was the late, great Carwyn James and it was his philosophy that was now being replayed at Stradey Park.

Although it was widely assumed that Gareth was the chief coach, with Allan playing a supporting role, the duo did not see it that way. Theirs was a partnership in the true sense of the word. Gareth assumed responsibility for the forwards preparing them both physically and mentally for battle while at the same time working on a strategy to adopt which would benefit the team. He was in charge of the juggernauts. Allan, on the other hand, took charge of the backs or the ballerinas. His job was to develop their potential, stimulate creativity and generally fine-tune what had been prepared on the practice field.

Whilst at Stradey Park, the pair's finest hour came on November 14th, 1992. The visitors were the World Cup holders, Australia. Even the most optimistic of supporters were in no doubt of the significance of the occasion and of the task that lay ahead. The Wallaby side selected for the encounter was a strong one – no 'mid-week' side this. This was by way of a compliment to Llanelli, but the Australians were also desperate to win.

One of the all-time greats, David Campese, welcoming us to Rocks in Sydney.

From the kick-off, it was obvious what the Scarlets's intentions were. They were no respecters of reputations and the tackling from the outset was ferocious. Although Australia kept winning a steady supply of possession, they weren't able to play with the flair and gay abandon which had enabled them to conquer the rugby world. Simon Davies, the Llanelli centre, resembled a heat-seeking missile following Marty Roebuck wherever he appeared on the field. On more than one occasion when it seemed as if the Wallaby full-back had broken free, Davies, a constant shadow, was there to bring him down and thwart any potential move.

Another outstanding performamce among many in the Llanelli camp was that produced by Huw Williams at full-back. He was a late replacement for the injured Ian Jones, but took full advantage of the opportunity afforded him, and produced the performance of a lifetime. One particular incident stood out when in tackling Tim Horan, the Australian outside half, he lifted the Wallaby off his feet and dumped him unceremoniously head first into the mud.

The Scarlets pack played its socks off, with Phil Davies, Mark Perego and Emyr Lewis appearing to be supercharged for the confrontation. Only one try was scored during the game, and that a superb effort created by the home side. It came from a move perfected on the training paddock and once again demonstrated that sparkle which seems part and parcel of Llanelli's folklore. The catalyst was fly-half Colin Stephens. With ball in hand, he feigned on two occasions to release two teammates and in the process created a huge void for Ieuan Evans to exploit. The wing threequarter, appeared like a genie out of a lamp, received the ball at pace and darted over near the posts. The 15,000 crowd was on its feet, the try resulting in a cheer which could be heard from Kidwelly to Cynheidre.

With a minute left to the end of the match, the scoreboard read Australia 9 Llanelli 7. What followed could have been written by Tarantino or Spielberg – it was of such high drama. With the ball in hand Colin Stephens, completely ignoring urgent calls from his centres, decided to attempt a drop goal. Unfortunately, it proved not to be one of his better attempts and drew groans

Another score from that try machine, Ieuan Evans.

from the nervous spectators around the ground. However, as in all the best dramas there came a twist at the end. It is true that the ball was not well struck and its trajectory was questionable, but as everyone looked on in stunned silence, the ball just went on and on and then miraculously scraped over the bar. It was only when the referee raised his arm in confirmation that everyone realized the significance of the young man's effort.

The cheer that went up to greet the try was nothing compared with the eruption that greeted the announcement of the score: Llanelli 10 Australia 9. With his confidence now stratospheric, the outside-half added another drop goal for good measure The final result read Llanelli 13 Australia 9. There were fifteen heroes on display at Stradey Park that afternoon, but we must not forget the two magnificent coaches.

Scarlet to the core

(It was a fine summer's evening in May 2003 and some three hundred of us had gathered at the Diplomat Hotel in Llanelli for a testimonial dinner to honour the Scarlets wing threequarter and full-back, Garan Evans. The guest speaker was to be the inimitable Ray Gravell, and when he stood up to speak, a respectful silence immediately descended, turning a boisterous dining room into somehere which more resembled the Bodleian at Oxford.

What he had to say that evening left the listener both energized and emotional in equal parts. He had his audience transfixed (and this without an autocue or notepad in sight) – his use of both languages, English and Welsh, was a joy. He spoke from the heart. When Ray drew to a close, we all rose as one in appreciation of what we had just experienced.

Unfortunately, the media weren't present to record the event, but as soon as I arrived home I made some notes and the following is a brief transcript of what the great man had to say).

The media, like sportsmen and sportswomen, are all too fond of using soundbite cliches. For example – 'It is an honour and a privilege to be here' or 'He's one of

The Diabetes Society golf day at Machynys near Llanelli. The unassuming winger Garan Evans is the golfer, not me!

the best players of his generation'. These are just two examples of the ones most commonly used. The more sceptical or intelligent among you would have reason to assume that the speaker was only mouthing the words, and that he or she didn't really mean what was said.

Ladies and gentlemen, tonight, with my hand on my heart I can truly say that it is a pleasure and a great honour to be here at the Diplomat to thank a fellow Scarlet, a Welshman to the core, a close friend and a most genuine and sincere human being. Garan Evans's contribution to Llanelli Rugby Football Club is immeasureable.

The Scarlets are famous all over the world, and have produced some of the best players ever to play the game. Every decade a new name comes to the fore - Harry, Ernie, Albert, Ivor, RH, Terry, Ray, Carwyn, Delme, Barry, Phil, JJ, Derek, Jonathan, Ieuan, Scott, Stephen and Dwayne. Every one of these was a hero at Stradey, but they also managed to conquer the rugby world. Just think back to 1959 when the All Blacks themselves described R.H. Williams as one of the best second-row forwards in world rugby. The magnificent Colin Meads was a man of few words, but this is what he had to say about RH. 'If R.H. Williams had been born in New Zealand, he would have been a permanent fixture in an All Blacks XV.' This was the sentiment echoed in South Africa too, where RH outplayed van Wyk, Claassens and du Rand.

Now Garan would be the first to admit that he doesn't fall into quite the same category! But one thing he does possess in spades is loyalty and in an age where players move from club to club chasing money, the young man from Penmynydd near Trimsaran has stayed true to his roots. From the time when he took his first steps he came to Stradey to watch the team play and the thought of playing for another club was something he could never contemplate. Even during a lean patch, when he seemed to spend most of his time on the bench, he was never tempted to sign for another club. His attitude was positive – he would improve his game and fight for his place so that he could wear the Scarlet jersey again.

In 1998 the auburn-haired youngster was selected for the Welsh squad to tour southern Africa. He was ecstatic when he was selected to play for his country against South Africa at Pretoria but as history reminds us, it was Wales's worst ever defeat, with the Springboks winning 96-13. Garan, like other team members, hung their heads in shame. This match would be the last for many of the players and, for four long years, many were ignored by the Welsh coaches and selectors. For a period he joined the class of 'one-cap wonders'.

These weren't good times for Garan, because not only was the humiliation of the tour still on his mind, but he also suffered from a series of minor injuries. A lesser man would have thrown in the towel but not Garan – it was not his way. He was determined to get himself fit and play once more for the Scarlets and Wales. He was out to prove that he was a better player than the one on view in Pretoria!

During the last few seasons at Llanelli, Garan has proved his point. He has distinguished himself at full back and wing threequarter – Mr Dependable himself. He is a natural footballer, quick off the mark, safe in defence, an accurate kicker of a ball and someone who is rare these days, an individual who can read the game. More importantly, he is a genuinely nice person which makes him a firm favourite at Stradey Park and beyond.

His success at Stradey was followed in 2002/03 with a trip to Australia and New Zealand and then a second cap at Lansdowne Road, Dublin, where he crowned a marvellous performance with an excellent try. How did he do it? How did he bring himself back from the brink? Well, of course he has the talent, but I would say it has more to do with character, guts and determination.

I happened to be present at St Helen's in Swansea in 1990 when Garan scored a memorable try against the Jacks. Let me remind you of what happened. Scott Gibbs was attacking on the Llanelli 22, and with the huge white-jerseyed forwards on the rampage, the alarm bells were ringing for the Scarlets. However, inexplicably Llanelli won the ball – Rupert Moon went to the blind side and fed Frano Botica who was under enormous pressure. He managed a miraculous pass out to Garan who decided to counter-attack.

The right wing wearing a distinctive red headband, veered inside and then outside to completely outwit Mark Taylor . . . his innate ability came to the fore – he seemed to be toying with the opposition. And then, in an instant, he changed gear, sprinting effortlessly along the touchline with the Swansea backs giving chase. It was too late; he crossed undeneath the posts for a truly spectacular try. St Helen's has witnessed many great tries and Garan's has to be amongst the best.

Ladies and gentlemen, a toast if you please to Garan Evans, one who rightly deserves his place amongst the Scarlet greats – a true and faithful servant.

S4C's *Codi Canu* – a competition between the respective choirs of the four Welsh regions. I was captain of the Scarlets' choir. That's why the Dragons won!

Sorry, Mari

(The following is an anecdote taken from a speech Ray delivered during his tesimonial dinner at the Stradey Park Hotel on Sunday, July 15th, 2007.)

Seeing Gareth, Gerald, Mervyn, and Jack here tonight brings back happy memories of that unforgettable day in France in 1975. And not forgetting of course J.J. Williams – the best person I have had the pleasure of sharing a room with. Sorry Mari!

East is best

I count myself fortunate in many ways, as rugby football was different from all other sports. Let me explain. During the eighty minutes on the field of play, scenes could very often resemble war zones – no prisoners taken or given on either side. The physical contact was brutal, the tackling remorseless and I dread to think what went on between the forwards at scrum, ruck and maul.

Then, when the final whistle blew everything changed, we shook hands as we left the playing arena and almost immediately the socializing began. This was the case at the end of every match and was even the norm at that most hostile of arenas, Pontypool Park!

The Golden Oldies meeting up at the Marriott Hotel in Cardiff. Or, as Mary Hopkin, would have said: 'Those were the days'.

Now I took my friendship with Roy, Phil, Delme and Gareth for granted because I spent a great deal of time in their company, but the same could not be said of Graham. Charlie and Bobby. However, once we'd showered and had made our way to the clubhouse, we greeted each other like long-lost friends.

I have to say that years later I was over the moon to hear that Luke and Sean Windsor had attended Welsh-medium schools in Gwent. Their father, Bobby Windsor, had played hooker for the British Lions in 1974 when the mighty Springboks were comprehensively beaten in the test series. He had also featured in the Grand Slam successes in 1976 and 1978. Bobby was born and brought up in Cross Keys in a period when the Welsh language was rarely heard in the Gwent valleys. Forty years later there has been a resurgence in the fortunes of the language of heaven with Welsh-language schools dotted all over the south-east, including ones in Newport, Abergavenny, and even in the shadow of the Severn Bridge.

I'd like to think that those occasions I spent quietly pointing out the advantages of a bilingual education to Bobby as well as many hours of playing Dafydd Iwan tapes on buses and changing rooms had borne fruit! Bobby Windsor is one of many parents who is proud that his children attended Ysgol Gymraeg Bryn Onnen and Ysgol Gyfun Gwynllyw in Pontypool. As I always said, 'After West – East is best! C'mon the Pooler!'

What a stupid question!

Those friends who know me well will testify that I'm not the most confident of men – that I always seek reassurance for whatever I say or do. This may extend from the rugby field to a radio or television interview, or even when the director signals the end of a shoot. I will always ask, 'How did I perform?'

During my playing days I now realize that I must have driven my fellow players mad in the dressing room prior to kick-off. The questions would always be the same, 'Who's the best centre in Wales?' or 'Who's the strongest and best-looking rugby player in the Northern Hemisphere?' They were childish questions, but it was all part of the ritual I had to go through before every game.

There was one occasion during the 1980 Lions tour of South Africa when I really plumbed the depths of stupidity. I was sharing a room with Jeff Squire, the beefy number eight from Pontypool, and he wasn't greatly impressed when, at six o'clock in the morning, I woke him up with the immortal words, 'Jeff, did I sleep all right?'

The Best Centre in Wales

Scores of my fellow players will hopefully testify to my warm-hearted, engaging personality. They will also be aware, however, of my lack of confidence just before kick-off. As will a host of referees! Especially those who visited the changing rooms to check the players' studs, because some officials were suddenly grabbed, literally by the throat and challenged 'Who is the best centre in Wales?' 'Who is the strongest centre in Wales?' This was a weekly ritual I had to perform to prepare myself psychologically for the ensuing encounter.

One anecdote perfectly illustrates this pre-match preparation. The rugby season was drawing to its close, and Llanelli and Bridgend were competing for the top slot in the *Western Mail's* unofficial championship table. I was pacing around the visitors' dressing-room at the Brewery Field like a caged lion, the same questions were again and again asked of my fellow team members, 'Who's the most creative centre in Wales?' 'Who is the most attractive player in world rugby?' 'JJ, who's the most destructive centre in rugby history?' Again the answers were the same – 'You, Ray!'

Some ten minutes into the game, a scrum formed on the halfway line, and the ball shot out into my hands. Spying the tiniest of openings between Steve

JJ (left) and Gareth. Two great athletes.

Fenwick and Lyndon Thomas, I shot past the two Bridgend defenders like a bat out of hell. I then raced downfield for some 30 metres, drew an opponent and passed the ball to the supporting J.J. Williams. With just 15 metres to sprint to the try-line, a Llanelli score was inevitable. Unfortunately for the Scarlets, they had not reckoned on the speedy response of Bridgend's J.P.R. Williams. The full-back's immense physical presence and his ability to cause grown men to tremble after one of his bone-shuddering tackles were legendary. But he was also fleet of foot and like a tiger chasing its prey, he launched himself at JJ bringing him down to ground just inches short of the try-line.

It was obvious that poor J.J. Williams was in a great deal of pain as a result of the encounter. I was first on the scene. 'Quick, Ray. Get Bert Peel. I'm in severe pain. I think I might have broken my collar bone.' The reply was a little unusual and not the one the injured winger was expecting to hear. 'Yes, yes, yes, JJ. All in good time. But who's the best centre in Wales?'

4

On Air

Paris

The twenty-five or so years I spent as a member of the BBC and S4C rugby commentary team were some of the happiest days of my life. When your working day is spent in the company of friends, nothing seems to be too much trouble – and this group of people certainly became close colleagues. Take Rhydian John, the floor manager – he could pass as a bouncer or bodyguard any day. Then there was Siôn Thomas, the producer (now I could write a book or two about Sioni's escapades), Rhys Edwards, Richard Bartley the cameraman and my very good friend from the Swansea valley, Geraint Rowlands.

A gang from Tumble decide to go to Paris in 2007 dressed as ... Grav!

During the international season when Wales played away from home, our 'weekend' would often start on the Wednesday before the match. This early start was necessary because the executives on the third floor wanted some titbits, and interesting pieces to camera as part of the pre-match preparations. Of course, my friends and neighbours in the Gwendraeth valley did not understand the need for this early start and they never failed to tease me with comments such as 'Off to Paris on Wednesday Grav – what a life you lead!' or 'The BBC and S4C have got more money than sense!'

But honestly it was hard work. First of all we had to choose locations; then get permission to film, and every now and then, in the middle of a shot, we'd be moved along by the *gendarmes*, and have you ever tried speaking to a camera from the top of the Eiffel Tower in a high wind! When we had finished filming for the day we then had to pack everything carefully away, pile into two taxis and rush back to the hotel so that the hours of film could be edited to the three minutes or whatever the producer required. Of course, I was never completely happy with my takes, and was always asking, 'Was that OK?' or 'How was the voice?' or 'Do you need another take?'

After a few seasons, these cameos of mine were dubbed 'Grav's Travels' and became part of the international day build-up. I was so proud to be part of the whole production that I would have done whatever was asked of me. I would go as far as to say that if Ger had asked me to dive into the Seine in my scarlet underpants, I would have done so immediately!

One particular weekend in Paris lingers in the memory to this day. It was 1995, the twentieth anniversary of my first cap at Parc des Princes. To celebrate the occasion, the team (and by team here I mean the production team) wanted to recreate a scenario which had taken place in 1975 and which I had described on many occasions.

As we ran out onto the field that Saturday afternoon in January 1975, the 75,000 or so supporters were chanting 'MASO! MASO! MASO!' I knew that

C'est Jo Maso! (far right).

the Narbonne centre wasn't playing that day – so why were they all shouting his name? I went up to Gareth and Gerald before singing the respective national anthems and said, 'My God! If they're shouting like this for a centre who isn't playing, then the midfield partnership of Dourthe and Bertranne must be world beaters!' (I was later told that the crowd were so incensed that Jo Maso wasn't selected that they chanted his name throughout the match).

We managed to recreate the events of 1975 (with the help of sound effects) from outside the stadium. Then it was a mad dash to Notre Dame, the Arc de Triomphe and Place de la Concorde before crossing over to the left bank to complete the filming. We didn't have time for an espresso or a cappuccino, let alone a stop for a leisurely French lunch.

When the producer eventually shouted 'Wrap!' we were completely exhausted and glad to arrive at the restaurant at the Concorde St Lazare for a hearty dinner. The hotel foyer was buzzing with past players and rugby aficionados. Most of the players on the concourse were from my rugby-playing days and I was flattered when I received several invitations to join them for dinner. Surprisingly, as it may seem, I declined. I now found myself to be more comfortable in the company of the BBC crew or with the fans rather than spend the evening reminiscing with former players.

After dinner the crew decamped to the bar for a few glasses of red wine (and an occasional brandy) and at one o'clock in the morning, just as I was about to say *bon soir*, out of the corner of my eye I caught sight of a familiar profile. The shock of curly hair and the wire-framed spectacles could belong to only one person and yes, it was him – one of the best centre threequarters to have played the game, Jo Maso.

As our eyes met, he sprang to his feet and shouted,

On the way to the commentary box.

'*C'est Ray Gravell!*' With arms outstetched he ran towards me, hugged me warmly and kissed me on both cheeks. Now, as we had never met before, I was a little taken aback that this icon of French rugby had recognized me. Just imagine, Joe Maso had acknowledged me at one o'clock in the morning in a hotel bar in France. When I eventually made it to my bed, the hotel staff were busily preparing for *le petit dejeuner*. I didn't tell him that he was part of the S4C pre-match entertainment!

From *Ar Grwydr 'da Grav* ('Grav's Travels') S4C, 1995.

If Not, Mynyddygarreg, Where?

If I were to ask you, where you'd want to spend your last day, and it couldn't be anywhere in Wales, where would that be? After all, you're a much travelled man?

I wouldn't go far – just sixty miles across the water, the Irish Sea – Ireland, or Erin. I first went there during the 1974/75 season – England and Wales were playing Scotland and Ireland in a special match to celebrate the Irish centenary. We were staying at the Shelbourne Hotel, a magnificent hotel with all its history and tradition, including the signing of the Treaty in 1922. I was aware of all things Irish, but I'd never been there before. I had this strange feeling during that first visit – I was away from home but I felt at home and for a number of years I kept asking the question, 'Why do I feel this way?' I return regularly; in fact, we visit, as a family, on a regular basis.

Matchday: (from the left) me, former Welsh captain and fellow summarizer Gwyn Jones and his brother Rhys, and Welsh-language presenter Gareth Roberts.

Do you think that we, the Welsh, are more similar to the Irish than any other country?

I think so. There's an affinity, there's a similarity, there's a closeness. It's more than a Celtic thing. I really feel at ease in the Republic and by now we have many close friends.

What about Irish music? Are you tuned into the scene?

Definitely. I've met Christy Moore a few times and, on one occasion, he caught hold of me and squeezed me as if we were opponents on a rugby field. He's just a lovely man. I love his music and what it conveys. Also The Fureys. Sadly, on August 14th 1990, my mother passed away – a terrible day for us as a family. The bouquets of flowers arrived at Brynhyfryd, in fact one bouquet was enormous, the biggest I've ever seen in my life, about six feet in height and from The Dubliners – Ronnie Drew and Eamonn Campbell! The greeting was significant, a Dublin saying stating simply, 'Keep her going Patsy.'

The Final Curtain
with Max Boyce
(BBC Radio Wales)

With two good friends and fellow Welsh-language presenters, MarciG and Sian Thomas.

The Emerald Isle

(A personal view of Dublin and the Irish people as presented by Ray on the daily magazine programme Heno *on S4C on the eve of the Ireland v Wales international in 2000)*

It's the landscape, it's the people, the Guinness and Dublin's fair city which attracts the tourists in their hundreds of thousands to the Emerald Isle. Once you arrive, the warmth of the welcome from the Irish people means you never, ever want to leave. This weekend, it's the game that has brought everyone here to the banks of the Liffey. If you happen to be wearing green or red, the enthusiasm is just the same.

There are now approximately two million people living in Dublin and a large percentage of those are under 25. It's easy to understand why the city is so dynamic and so full of life. If any country has benefited from European funding, it's Ireland – you can see from the large amount of building work going on, and the fact that 'unemployment' is a word seldom heard. There certainly seems to be a buzz along O'Connell Street, St Stephen's Green, Grafton Street and the Temple Bar area. The place is full of bars, restaurants, and clubs – it truly is a cosmopolitan city.

(During a piece to camera in the middle of Lansdowne Road, into shot comes the groundsman waving his arms and shouting, 'Get off the grass immediately.' He then spots Ray and for the next twenty minutes it's 'Ray, what can I do for you?' and 'Everything OK Ray?')

Here we are at Lansdowne Road – and boy, oh! boy what a place! I still remember the first time I played on the hallowed turf back in 1974 – ah! the memories come flooding back as if it was yesterday. It's a strange sort of place, intimidating yet friendly. There's something unique about playing the Irish – you feel as if you're up against fifteen banshees and when those Garryowens go up, then it's time to offer a little prayer and hope for the best.

This ground is the oldest on the Six Nations circuit – Wales played here back in 1882, and not much has changed since then, but it still keeps a lot of its charm. You can walk here comfortably from the city centre in about half an hour or you can take the local rail link, called the Dart. In fact the railway runs directly under the West Stand, so you can get off the train and walk straight into your seat.

(Outside the ground a huge poster advertises the forthcoming Six Nations Championship. Depicted on it are the six national captains with Keith Wood at the front holding a rugby ball under his right arm. Not so obvious are the features of the five other captains, and Ray cannot resist referring to this in his remarks).

We are now standing outside the ground and behind me you can see this huge poster advertising the season's international matches. We can all recognise Keith Wood, but to me the Welsh captain looks like Max Boyce. Now I know that Graham Henry is reshuffling his team but does he honestly intend including the superstar from Glynneath in his line-up for Saturday? We'll have to wait and see!

(For his next piece to camera, Ray positions himself outside one of Dublin's most prestigious hotels.)

So where does the Irish team stay when the big matches are staged in Dublin? The answer is the Berkeley Court Hotel, which is just a stone's throw from the ground. All the stars stay there when they're in town – U2, Bewitched, Boyzone, Peter O'Toole and Richard Harris. You name them and they've stayed here. I can tell you one thing, you need their bank account to be able to stay at the Berkeley Court – either that or win the lottery!

Commissionaire: Ray, is it the Rolls or the Bentley?
Ray: John, we're in Dublin. I'll take the Dart.

On the morning of the match and Jury's in Ballsbridge is the only place to be (or, if you're lucky, inside Jury's at Ballsbridge). Lansdowne Road is only three hundred yards behind the hotel and the excitement is infectious. As far as I'm concerned, just sampling the atmosphere brings out the goosepimples. And another thing, if you're looking for a ticket you might just be lucky enough to find one, but not from a ticket tout. Don't be fooled by them, they'll charge you a fortune!

(Ray insists of re-living the past and retires to the lounge of the Shelbourne Hotel.)

There are hundreds of hotels in Dublin but my all time favourite is the Shelbourne. It's an old building and stands proudly behind St Stephen's Green, steeped in tradition and romance and here's a little tip. It serves the best afternoon tea in Dublin. *(His statement to the camera is suddenly interrupted.)*

Mary: Are you, by any chance, Ray Gravell who played for Wales back in the seventies?

Ray: Well, yes. I'm surprised you recognized me.

Mary: Mr Gravell – this is your bill which is outstanding since 1974.

Ray: O! Mary fach!

I first stayed here in the 1970s when I was playing for Wales and have been back and forth every year since. You never know who you'll bump into in the foyer – last night I met Ronnie Wood from the Rolling Stones.

Dublin is a city which is proud of its culture and rightly so with people of the calibre of W.B. Yeats, Jonathan Swift, George Bernard Shaw and Patrick Kavanagh. *(Ray stands on a pavement on Pembroke Road and recites a few lines from Kavanagh's poem, 'If you ever go to Dublin Town'):*

On Pembroke Road look out for my ghost,
Dishevelled with shoes untied.
Playing through the railings with little children
Whose children have long since died.

There is a huge amount of respect for Kavanagh's work in Ireland, especially his poem about the potato famine. The work raised a few eyebrows when it was written but the message it contained could not be disputed.

The list of literary greats goes on, but one of the giants was James Joyce – some say he was the best writer since Shakespeare. Most people are familiar with the *Dubliners* and *Finnegan's Wake* but his most famous work was *Ulysses*. What Joyce set out to do was write a novel describing Dublin in such a way that if the city was suddenly destroyed, it could be rebuilt using the book as a reference.

For anyone interested in the life of James Joyce, a visit to Sandycove near Dún Laoghaire is a must. And when you get there you must go to the Martello Tower, the home of his friend Oliver St John Gogarty (Buck Mulligan in the novel). Here in 1904 Joyce spent his last week in Ireland before he left the country for good with his love, Nora Barnacle.

Dublin has two canals – the Royal and the Grand. The Grand was built as a means of communicating the city with the surrounding countryside. They were such an important means of transport that even when the railways arrived the canals remained busy. It is said by the locals that any true Dubliner is born between the two canals.

Theobald Wolfe Tone was a hero of the nineteenth century, a barrister by profession and a member of the Irish Protestant Church. He preached equal rights for Protestants and Catholics in Ireland and there is no doubt that if the politicians had heeded his words then all the sectarian violence which has dogged the country could have been avoided. The world needs more politicians like Tone.

(Wales defeated Ireland 23-19 at Lansdowne Road on April 1st, 2000)

OOPS!

I know I should have paid more attention during the English Language classes at Queen Elizabeth Grammar School, Carmarthen, but honestly I never thought that I would ever meet anyone bearing the title 'Viscount' in Mynyddygarreg.

The occasion for my mistake took place on the Radio Wales programme *Streetlife* during the 1980s. On the morning in question, a written note came from the producer requesting me to wish George Thomas, or Viscount Tonypandy, a happy birthday. I was happy to do so, and conveyed our sincere wishes to the Vi**s**count. Within seconds, a voice came bellowing down the headphones, 'Ray, for goodness' sake, it's Vi(s)count Tonypandy – don't pronounce the "S"!' Correct your mistake immediately or the Director General of the BBC in London will be in touch.

Without another thought, I uttered the immortal line, 'Listeners, can I apologise for my earlier mistake. I should have said Vicount not Vi**s**count but somebody has spelt it V-I-S-C-O-U-N-T on this card in front of me!'

As presenters of *Street Life* on BBC Radio Wales, Frank Hennessy and I always had great fun. Pity he couldn't have given me lessons in pronunciation, mind!

GRAVELISM

(BT and Vodaphone loved Grav. His landline and mobile would be red-hot all day long, as the Mynyddygarreg Exocet rang Wayne, his Carmarthen bookie, Pinky, Tomos Morse, Les, Robert, Keith Bach, MarciG, Siôn and Geraint Rowlands)

Geraint: Grav, I've got to go. We'll have a chat later.

Grav: Before I go . . . how's your mam?

Geraint: Great, Grav. She's on good form.

Grav: Tip-top, Ger. Remember, you only get one mam.

The Grav show back live on air from Stradey Park. The team (from the left) is MarciG, Keith Bach, Ffion Hywel, Tomos Morse and me.

5

The Peacemaker

The Braveheart of the Gorsedd Circle

I thought I was dreaming when I received a phone call from Dafydd Rowlands offering me the position of the ceremonial Sword Bearer of the Gorsedd of Bards at the National Eisteddfod. He said he'd discussed the idea with Meirion Evans and Hywel Teifi Edwards and they had both agreed it was an inspired choice, or so Dafydd claimed! I accepted immediately of course. To be perfectly honest the offer gave me just as much pleasure as the first cap I'd won for Wales.

Much later Hywel Teifi told me, 'Grav, you can be a kind of Eisteddfod Braveheart!'

'Hywel,' I replied, 'I'd rather to be Glyndŵr.'

In the foyer of City Hall in Cardiff in the company of my great hero – Owain Glyndŵr.

Red Hand and *Cawl*

(*In conversation with Max Boyce*).

Who would you spend your last day with?

He's from the past, but his legacy lives on in the present. Max, he's still with us!

O'i loches yn Eryri,	(From his refuge in Eryri
Fe ddaw â'i ffyddlon lu,	He will lead his loyal troops
I'n harwain gyda'r wawr	To herald the free Wales
I'r Gymru rydd.	At break of day.)

Dafydd Iwan's words about Owain Glyndŵr, the only man to unite the whole of Wales albeit, sadly, for only two years. Approximately six hundred years ago they burnt his house down at Sycharth but this man was a visionary, a scholar, a linguist and a diplomat – he'd served at the Inns of Court, served in the court of Henry IV; he was a nobleman, had all the riches. He didn't need to fight or bicker with anybody, he had everything seemingly that he wanted. However, his dream was for his nation to be a nation – a united nation, with a university and a church to represent the people. Today's assembly, the *Cynulliad*, is a recent development but Owain formed his own assembly – to say he was ahead of his time would be an understatement. I would love to spend the day with him, preferably attacking the invaders down near Kidwelly Castle as he did. I would die for that man.

You played Owain Glyndŵr's nephew, Owain Lawgoch ('Owain of the Red Hand') in a drama documentary. I saw you on horseback wearing chainmail. How did you feel being transported back to the fourteenth century in charge of boiling oil?

The whole thing was a great experience. I was a bit worried initially as the horse was a bit frisky. I just felt the part, my mind went back to the period. I read lots of books about Owain – his ideals and his philosophy are still alive, being implemented and put in place. His spirit lives on in Wales.

What meal are you going to choose for Owain? I'm expecting you to order venison, wild boar or even swan stuffed with wigeon.

That's more for Henry VIII. I'm sure Owain would go along with this. It's definitely *cawl* for starters because the great bards of the fourteenth century such as Iolo Goch sang for Owain, '*Na syched byth yn Sycharth*' – there'll never be any thirst in Sycharth, one of Owain's homes. But I would have *cawl* because *cawl* to me fed the imagination, fuelled the creativity of these great bards. So we must begin with a bowl of *cawl*, Max. I absolutely love *cawl* – my mother used to make *cawl pys*.

Cawl with lamb, Ray?

Lamb or beef or *cawl pys* with just peas. My father loved *cawl pys* more than any other *cawl* and I yearn for *cawl*. Mari's Auntie Gwyneth makes me *cawl* and my Auntie Barbara (dad's younger sister). Mari as yet hasn't perfected the art – I live in hope! But we would begin with a bowl of *cawl* each.

The Final Curtain

Enjoying my week at the Eisteddfod.

More Important than the Lions

Like everybody else on God's earth, I'm delighted when somebody writes in praise of me. There's nothing better for a player's mental state than to read favourable reports in the press. Mind you, I wasn't one to buy the papers on a regular basis – the *Llanelli Star*, the *South Wales Evening Post* and the *Western Mail* didn't arrive on my doorstep at daybreak, but when a friend or relative mentioned some positive article or other, I used to make every effort to nip down the newsagent's and buy a copy. I realized, during my career as a centre with Llanelli and Wales, that it was impossible for rugby correspondents to please everybody. Every now and again they would have to criticize, and players are quite prepared to accept such criticism if it is levelled constructively and is a fair reflection of what has occurred on the pitch. Often, the best criticism is silence!

I would have been a useless reporter – my instinct was always to expect the best from a player not concentrate unduly on his weaknesses. As a summarizer in the company of Huw Llywelyn Davies and Wyn Gruffydd, I used to love waxing lyrical in praise of a well-constructed team try, but words eluded me when a winger knocked the ball on with the try-line at his mercy. I was speechless when the Scarlets lost three Heineken Cup semi-finals – some, who should have known better, searched for explanations and found fault with the players and coaches. But I looked at the positives and congratulated everyone that we had come so close – within a whisker of winning the cup.

During the last few seasons, I've been given the opportunity to compile columns for the Scarlets' match-day programme and have found the experience a rewarding one – looking forward not back, as we all will have to in the next

S4C promo – Chris Wyatt typecast as the barman; Wyn Gruffydd and I ordering lemonades and, honest now, Mari, I don't know who the blonde is!

few months and years. When plans for a new stadium in the town's Pemberton and Trostre area were revealed, I was disappointed because the old field had served generations of players. History is important. In a few months, Stradey will be no more; hundreds of houses will have been built on a piece of land that was the battlefield of Ernie, Albert, Ray, Carwyn, Delme, Norman, Phil, and thousands of other Scarlets. It's sad to think of it as Kidwelly castle continues as a reminder of the suffering and sacrifice of the past. But, there we are – we must get used it and look forward confidently to the future.

I have so many memories of the old days – a mind full of the past's reels of film. Some fill their cupboards with programmes, or newspaper cuttings neatly pasted into scrapbooks, whilst others have sizeable collections of videos containing memorable moves and tries. I'm not that organized! Mind you, when

I'm a little down, there is one essay about me that never fails to energize me; after reading it, I emerge from the shadows ready to face the giants of my forefathers!

In 2000, Professor Hywel Teifi Edwards and Gomer Press in Llandysul published another volume in that excellent series *Cyfres y Cymoedd* ('The Valleys Series'). This time, it was the Gwendraeth valley that was showcased, and it was decided that the Crowned Poet and Archdruid Dafydd Rowlands should be invited to contribute an essay about me. I counted this a privilege; it was an honour to share the limelight with the musicians, politicians, miners, authors, actors and people of the Gwendraeth valley – I felt I wasn't worthy of inclusion since it was on a football pitch that I had come to prominence.

After reading Dafydd's masterpiece, I was in tears, and for many reasons. Naturally I was chuffed that I was the subject of such a eulogy, but more importantly I felt that he had analysed my character perfectly as he compared me to other figures in a variety of fields. It isn't my intention to boast here; it's not that I feel myself a special individual, but I want to state emphatically that Dafydd Rowlands, like some high-flying psychiatrist in a clinic, had succeeded to articulate the character and personality of Raymond Gravell of Mynyddygarreg.

Every now and again, I escape to the depths of Brynhyfryd to read his words.

> . . . Choosing him for that honoured position [of being the Gorsedd's Sword Bearer] was inspired, and Ray himself has said that accepting the post was as great a thrill as some of those thrills he experienced when he was chosen to play for Wales and when Llanelli beat the All Blacks in 1972. I remember well the day that Grav carried the Sword in the Bridgend Eisteddfod's Proclamation procession. He had flown back specially from South Africa to carry out his Gorsedd duties, and during our dignified march through the streets of Bridgend, Ray was greeted by

the hundreds who lined the route. They had seen fiery flashes of him on the Brewery Field many times, and thought the world of him. As Archdruid at the time, I was walking behind Ray and hearing all that the crowd was saying as we went past. And I remember most distinctly hearing someone shout 'Ray! Why aren't you in South Africa with the Lions?' The response was immediate – 'This is more important!' I have been privileged enough to walk behind him several times by now, and have noticed one thing especially – the Sword Bearer attracts more

Holding the Sword of Peace aloft with the Archdruid, Dafydd Rowlands (right), and the Recorder, John Gwilym Jones.

attention than the Archdruid himself. When we marched through Llanelli a year ago, the same thing happened – everyone calling Ray's name. Many in the crowd didn't know what they were witnessing – like the young mother who answered her child's enquiry about what all this meant: 'I'm not sure, bach. I think it's got something to do with proper Welsh'.

Ray Gravell? Yes, 'proper Welsh'! Ray of the Mountain. Not any old mountain, but Mynyddygarreg. One of the sons of the Gwendraeth. He played 485 times for Llanelli, 23 times for Wales, and in four tests for the Lions. And he was fired up in every one of those games. He is still fired up, and is still singing the patriotic anthems, and shedding emotional tears. He will never be different, thank heavens.

What ever will be will be

(A conversation held between Ray and Robin McBryde at Brynhyfryd a few weeks before the Flintshire Eisteddfod 2007)

Ray: Dyfrig Roberts and John Gwilym Jones came to see me while I was in hospital and told me that the Eisteddfod Council had decided to ask you to carry the sword during my unavailability. I have to say I was over the moon when I heard the news. Robin, I could have danced around the room; I thought to myself, there really is a God! I also heard Dic, the Archdruid-elect, say on radio that he hoped I would be at his side at Cardiff in 2008. It will certainly be a challenge for me, and if you don't mind, Robin, I sincerely hope to be there.

Robin: Of course I don't mind Ray.

Ray: Your very good health, Robin.

The Strongest Welshman

(The Flintshire National Eisteddfod, August 2007)

Sword Bearers both – Robin McBryde and me.

Mari: I'm so glad that we're here in Flint this year. I honestly didn't think we'd see the 2007 Eisteddfod. We've been coming to the Eisteddfod campus for ten years – ever since Ray was made Sword Bearer, and by now the children are happy to rove around with their friends, leaving me on my own.

Ray: *(Roving in a leisurely fashion around the campus and addressing the camera)* Robin's doing a great job. By now, and this is odd, I can look at the ceremony from the outside, so to speak, and realize its significance. *(Robin arrives)* I know you're a stong guy, the strongest Welshman but come here – *(embraces him in the French manner)* here's a well-deserved kiss for the Sword Bearer. You were fantastic – carrying the sword with such dignity!

(Robin leaves and Ray continues to rove) I received two offers in my life that I found impossible to refuse – one was to represent my country on the rugby field and the other was to represent my country through carrying the Gorsedd's great sword. The Sword Bearer – they can keep their CBEs, OBEs, MBEs and any other BEs, and I say this respectfully. I have been honoured, though I might not deserve it, but I accepted the call with pride!

Dafydd Rowlands and I present a tableau of disappointment at the Bridgend National Eisteddfod in 1998: the Bardic Chair has been withheld because none of the competitors was deemed a worthy winner.

An Unfulfilled Fantasy

I think I'm one of the luckiest people in the world. I played for my country but on one occasion I had an offer which I just couldn't refuse – to carry the Sword of Peace. Naturally, I accepted and I will assume that task until I drop or until they sack me. It's a great privilege, a real honour – I've played for Wales but I must admit I'm close to tears when the Archdruid asks the bard to rise during chairing, crowning or prose medal ceremonies. If only I had the ability to win the crown or the chair at the National Eisteddfod – I've also dreamt of performing at La Scala in Milan. 'Beware your dreams, they might come true.' I only wish!

And what about your pseudonym? I can see it Ray. The Archdruid on his feet in the pavilion, the lights cascading around the amphitheatre that is the Eisteddfod – members of the bardic circle approaching in robes with the words echoing around the auditorium, 'A wnaiff "Scarlet" sefyll ar ei draed?' (Will 'Scarlet' be upstanding?) Then you rise, acknowledging the tumultuous applause – you'd have to leave the sword behind!

It's something I've dreamt of. I constantly think about it. When Mererid Hopwood was acclaimed, it was history in the making – the first woman in eight hundred years to win the chair. History being created in front of my very eyes. I cried with joy and fulfilment sharing in someone else's happiness. That was unforgettable.

The *Final Curtain*, with Max Boyce.

An emotional moment for all concerned. Mererid Hopwood wins the Chair at the 2001 National Eisteddfod. The Archdruid is Meirion Evans.

'Derek Brockway, you are my sunshine!'

The roving reporter interviews Lord Cwmtwrch, Clive Rowlands and his wife, Margaret, on the eisteddfod field.

Trying to persuade the National Eisteddfod's Chief Executive, Elfed Roberts, to bring the great annual festival to Mynyddygarreg.

Meirion Evans promises me a Bardic Chair as long as he gets a Welsh shirt!

The first programme back – September 2007

6

Strength in Weakness

'Hell, this is serious . . .'

When I saw the specialist walking down the corridor, I thought – Hell, he looks like that American actor John Goodman, who was in *The Flintstones* film years ago . . . 'Yabadabadoo' – and that's how I greeted him . . . 'Yabadabadoo'! They took the bandage off my leg and looked at me, and said, 'This isn't good. In fact, this isn't good at all – we're going to theatre now.'

I heard the words, but they didn't seem to sink in. Mari was sitting next to me and she was like a rock. Then I understood – Hell, this is serious. But from then onwards, Hywel, and it's quite strange: to me, everything was comparatively easy, but poor Mari – she was the one who had to put up with the situation; she had to walk out to the car park on her own; she had to come back to Mynyddygarreg to meet the girls from school and tell them that Dad was about to have a serious operation and that he was probably going to lose his leg. How was she going to break that news to my two little girls?

Part of a conversation with Hywel Gwynfryn on BBC Radio Cymru.

Manon (on the left) and Gwenan lead me on to the field before the testimonial match between the Scarlets and Bath, August 2007.

'You're going home . . .'

I longed to hear the words – 'Ray, the doctors are pleased. They're ready for you to go home.' As a family, we were aware of that possibility, and had planned everything carefully. We'd have to bring one of the girls' single beds downstairs to the old bedroom because there was no way I'd be able to get up the stairs in a wheelchair! Over the years, the house had been totally renovated apart from the old room where Mam, Dad and I had spent hours together. It was more or less as it used to be, apart from the fact that we'd plastered and papered a few walls.

And this would be Raymond Gravell's room for the next few weeks; a room full of fond memories. How on earth had we managed to fit so much furniture into such a small place? We had had a piano, a dining table, four chairs, a couch, a gramophone and a cupboard. Mam couldn't read music but she had a good ear and if she heard something that she liked, that would be it. Bang! She'd get on the piano, and play it totally by ear – and Dad would react straight away; on his feet, hitting those notes and singing away in his beautiful baritone voice. You know, in the deep deep silence of Glangwili Hospital late at night – and silence can be incredibly profound – I could hear a noise in the background. Yes, I'm telling you, Mam and Dad were there, singing away to entertain me.

There would always be music playing at home. Whenever Dad had the chance, the 78s would be on the old gramophone and the voices of Richard Rees and David Lloyd could be heard soaring over Mynyddygarreg. But remember, Jac and Wil – the two brothers from the Tumble – were my father's favourites. Dad loved them. I can still hear the voices of those passionate tenors, Enrico Caruso and Tito Schipa, as well as songs such as 'Ave Maria', 'Che Gelida Manina' or 'Pwy fydd yma mewn can mlynedd'. Usually there would be a great big coal fire in the grate, with the best coal in the world – beautiful, shiny anthracite coal from the Gwendraeth Valley. I was a young boy at the time, and

I'd often think when Dad was singing away, right in front of the fire, 'He's going to set his trousers on fire any minute!'

And yes, the news came. 'Ray. You're going home tomorrow!' Everyone had to shift pretty quickly to make sure that my room was ready for me. In the period I stayed in that room, I slept like a log, and I can't fathom why. You see, upstairs, I slept like a butcher's dog, and kept tossing and turning without being able to settle at all. I was desperate to be back upstairs with Mari; mentally, I was happier in her company. Despite that, the most important thing of all was being back home – the first chapter in the latest stage of my life.

A week has gone by since I've returned home and I must say that Nurse Ratched is doing a remarkable job. Who is Nurse Ratched? Well, Mari, the wife, of course! She is Nurse Ratched and that's the nickname I've given her. Nurse Ratched was the matron in the legendary American film, *One Flew over the Cuckoo's Nest*. Jack Nicholson had the starring role, and Michael Douglas was the producer. You film buffs will remember that the film is set in a mental hospital where the patients are infinitely wiser than the staff. Nurse Ratched was a strong and determined woman who didn't take any nonsense. Nonetheless, she had a heart of gold.

My personal Nurse Ratched makes sure that I take my medication on time. To be honest, Mari and I are used to it because I've had diabetes for seven years now. We had to keep it under control and be careful with my diet, but then suddenly, my glucose levels rocketed and I had to start using medication – two tablets first thing in the morning and two in the evening to control the disease. And Mari kept an eagle eye on things and since coming home my appetite is much better and that's very reassuring.

I've been going on and on about coming home last week, but I'm fully aware of all the help I had at Glangwili Hospital. They've been fantastic. On news bulletins, on the radio and television, they always focus on negative things; such and such is to blame for negligence and lack of care and so on. Why don't producers concentrate on good news once in a while? Why don't they tell the world that hundreds of thousands of people get better against all the odds? Things often look very bleak, and families fear the worst, but thanks to medicine and good care, patients can – miraculously – get better. I can vouch for the exceptional skill of Glangwili's doctors – individuals under a lot of pressure, but who get remarkable results despite their difficult circumstances.

When I was in hospital, I lost my appetite – the smell of the ward and my general circumstances meant that the menu wasn't particularly appetising. But now, at home, things are different, with fruit, vegetables and healthy food – once I smell them I start craving them. After just a week, I felt stronger. I still crash into a few walls in my wheelchair, I still sleep downstairs, but in a few days I'm going over to the ALAC Centre at Morriston Hospital to have some physiotherapy, to strengthen this body of mine before getting my artificial leg. Then, I'll have to learn to walk again! I'm impatient, and nervous, but more than anything I'm really looking forward to it. A senior nurse from Morriston has already been over to the house, and she's pleased with the way that the wound is healing.

Sleeping is a problem. I've never felt so uncomfortable in my life. It's impossible to turn on my side as the bandaged part around the wound is so sensitive. So, I sleep on my back – flat on my back. Instinctively, in my sleep, I turn to the left or right, and as it's a single bed, Mari worries that I'm going to fall out. There's a quilt over the bed, which gives me some freedom to move.

People have been so kind. It's impossible for me to express in words what we feel as a family; friends from all over the world have wished me well, some of whom I've never met and not likely to meet either. There's a link between the people who've sent greetings – Welsh people from all over Wales as well as people from Ireland, France and the Southern Hemisphere and even Japan – and the oval ball is the link. What a wonderful world we live in! I was introduced to the game for the first time as a little boy in my pushchair by Uncle Ron and

Dad. Ron John was a full-back for Kidwelly – a talented player who played for Llanelli once or twice. On my birthday they bought me a pair of studs and a rugby ball – I'd only just started walking and the ball was bigger than me. And do you know what – I can still smell that ball; the strong smell of that old leather ball!

Hundreds of cards arrived – piles of them came at the same time; there are over a thousand cards in boxes in the front room. Cards from friends and colleagues, but most have been sent by total strangers, which is a real boost to me. Visitors knock on the door to wish me well, while I'm as weak as a kitten, extremely tired, and finding it difficult to respond. Nonetheless, I'm very grateful. 'Thanks' is only a little word; it's not enough, perhaps, but it's the only thing I can give.

Taking things for granted – I've been guilty of doing that over the years. By now, because of this illness, I've come to see that even the smallest things can be taxing and tiring. Making myself a cup of tea is difficult when I'm sitting in a chair. I'm on a totally different level – Mari is only five foot one and I'm used to looking down on her but by now I look up to her.

As I'm housebound, there's plenty of time to think and contemplate. The other day, it struck me that I've realized my father's dreams. One of his dreams was to return to live on the mountain – buy a little cottage, renovate it, and in time, turn it into a big posh house. Dad, if you can hear me – the house is a palace, and unlike all those wonderful houses you see in the *Western Mail* supplement on Saturday, the view from the patio outside is one of the most beautiful in the world.

When we moved as a family to Brynhyfryd, there wasn't a sewerage system and that's how it was until 1982 – when Mam and I lived there together. Today, we have plenty of lavatories in the house, and all the waste flows away towards Kidwelly. Dad would be thrilled with these amenities.

He had another dream too, and I fulfilled it out in Paris in 1975, a few years

The best view in the world – from Brynhyfryd's patio.

after his death. Although I wasn't happy to see him out on the sidelines when I played for the Gram in Carmarthen, I would have been on top of the world to see him out in the seating area at Parc des Princes when I was representing Wales for the very first time. But it wasn't to be.

When he was seventeen, Dad started working underground and worked as a miner from then on at collieries in Trimsaran, Carwe and Pentre-mawr in Pontyberem. Before then, he earned his living at local quarries. He had many interests – the garden was his pride and joy, and he also loved rugby and socialising for a few hours with a couple of pints after the match on Saturday night. He liked a few pints, and thinking about his physically demanding job in the coal seam and the continuous dangers he faced, I must say that he deserved a night out with his friends. But I soon realized, while listening to international games on the 'wireless', that he had great ambitions for his son, one of which was playing for Wales. Job done, Dad!

At the moment, I'm totally dependent on Mari. She takes me to the lavatory, she washes me, and it's as if these demands are increasing day by day. I'm desperate for a shower; to be able to wash my whole body, rather than bits of it at a time. There's a big pan on the kitchen table, hot water and soap to hand, and as I wash the upper parts, Mari concentrates on the rest of my body. It's a daily ritual, so that I can look and feel my best.

Memories flood back as I wash in the kitchen. Every Monday in the 1950s, Dad came home from the pit covered from head to toe in coal dust, and the old tin bath would be ready and waiting for him. Mam would have already boiled the water, and when Dad stepped through the door, she'd pour the water for him. I, as a young boy, would have the honour – the privilege, as he'd say – of scrubbing his back. He was a big, muscular man, and had a big square back dotted with freckles here and there. I felt like a real man when I washed his back! When the pit-head baths came to the colliery, I remember seeing an army of miners stepping into the showers, scrubbing each others' backs. I don't want to return to those days, but it's good to remember them. A journey back in time would be quite an experience. Thankfully, the old memory is as sharp as ever and the cameos are still vivid in my mind.

Brynhyfryd, April 30th 2007

I'm moving carefully towards the patio and I'm conscious of the wheelchair squeaking on the ramps underneath. By now, I'm totally dependent on the chair, and we had to have ramps installed so that I could move in and out of the house. I must say that these circumstances feel very strange to a centre who used to bulldoze through opponents in international rugby games!

At the moment, I'm looking out onto the lower part of the Gwendraeth valley; the views are spectacular. Whatever the weather – rain, gale-force wind, snow, mist or warm sunshine – it's a fantastic panorama; the images are so different every day. It's what makes this part of the world so special. You can see Carmarthen Bay and take in the view right up towards the ancient town of Kidwelly and beyond – a town that dates back to before the twelfth century.

Kidwelly Castle

Tenby

From the patio, I can see Kidwelly Castle and St Mary's Church before moving my gaze to the Gower and more specifically, Worm's Head, to the east. To the west on a clear day, you can see Caldey Island. We can't see Tenby from here, but if we went down to the village we could catch a glimpse of the loveliest sea-side town in the world.

Underneath Brynhyfryd, the course of the Gwendraeth Fach can be followed over to Kidwelly, where it joins the Gwendraeth Fawr which flows down from Trimsaran. A smile comes to my face as I see the fields of Gwenllian Farm, a stone's throw from the house. It's a view that ignites my imagination; it's held a special significance for me since my childhood days, when I used to daydream about events that occurred near Gwenllian farmhouse and its lands. It was Dad that instilled this pride in me. He always preached about past glories. When we first moved here, in the mid 1950s, he told me the story of Princess Gwenllian. 'She was a gog [north Walian],' he said, 'a very beautiful girl – Gruffydd ap Pennant's daughter, who was married to Gruffydd ap Rhys, Lord of the South.'

He told me about her bravery and her sacrifice during an attack by the Normans on Kidwelly Castle, led by Maurice de Lambres. Think about it, Gwenllian was executed almost a thousand years ago in a bloody battle right underneath where I'm sitting at the moment. It was all woodland here at the time, and Gwenllian followed the river down to Kidwelly. Old stagers still talk about 'the river of blood' and the Welsh and the Normans who were killed in the massacre of 1136.

That happened almost a millennium ago, but believe me, her spirit is still here, and it still has a hold on generations of this area's inhabitants, as well as a strong presence in my mind. And it's my duty to pass on the history, and it's a rich history, to Manon and Gwenan – they must know about the history, culture and industrial background of their area. The past must be a part of their make-up.

The Story of my Illness

Why, tell me, am I babbling on like this, romanticizing the past? Because there was a time a few weeks ago when I thought that I'd never see this view again. The events of the past few weeks have been a totally unfamiliar experience to us as a family. I was suffering from diabetes as well as two other illnesses. There was a deficiency in the right leg – the blood supply wasn't going all the way down to the foot, and because of that, there were toxins in the tip of my little toe, and in about a week, it spread to the rest of the foot. My right foot was treated, and we hoped that the antibiotics would help. The doctors were hopeful that everything would be OK. Unfortunately, from my point of view, everything wasn't OK and I had to go to Glangwili Hospital in Carmarthen for emergency treatment, and I stayed there for six weeks.

In my private life, I've never been a person who looks back – today, tomorrow and the day after are what's important to me. But after a series of procedures, I realise that things are a bit different now – unreal to some extent – and I must admit that I'm feeling emotional, very emotional. The wheelchair's clocking up a few miles around the house but I'd like to stress that I'm happy with my world. I only just made it, and I'm eternally grateful to the specialist. He had to make a quick decision to save my life and he had to amputate the leg. Every minute of every hour in hospital I was desperate to go home – there's no place like home, and it's so very true. It takes an illness or an accident or a disability to make us really consider the values around us – values connected to the family, the locality, numerous friends and dear neighbours. Recently, I've had time to think and to re-live the past, memories have come flooding back, and I've come to the conclusion that another thing is very true – west is best!

After a few tests, I was given the news that I'd have to have the right leg amputated on April 13th, and on a Friday of all days! But, the number thirteen has always been very lucky for me because it's the number that I used to wear on the back of my scarlet Llanelli shirt, Wales's red shirt, the Lions shirt, the black and white shirt of the Barbarians and the multi-coloured shirt of Carmarthenshire. Having said that, when I crossed for a try for the Lions against the Springboks in Cape Town in 1980, I didn't have any number at all on my back – the original number-thirteen shirt had been torn off my body when I was lying at the bottom of a ruck.

The news was unexpected and a bit of a shock, but I reacted positively because there was no other choice – I agreed with the surgeon's decision. That's what saved my life. I had the operation on the Saturday and woke up in Glangwili's Intensive Care Unit, and thought that I'd passed onto another world. There were only six beds in the ward, and every patient was seriously ill. I wasn't fully aware of what was going on around me because of the drugs that were being pumped into my body to eradicate the poison that had decomposed my

It's a well-established tradition that Llanelli and Bath do battle for the rag doll – and here she is!

foot and was making its way around my body. There were many different poisons to kill – one of which was septicaemia, which is powerful enough to kill a horse. But the staff at Glangwili were wonderful – the specialist told me that he was just doing his job. That's what I call a job-and-a-half!

Slowly, I started to realize, after going back to the general ward, that life had changed considerably for Raymond Gravell, and everything had happened overnight too. But after tossing and turning for a while, trying to put things in perspective, I decided that life was still sweet – it's good to be here. Out here on the patio in Brynhyfryd, I'm still optimistic and I think about positive things and push away any negative thoughts.

Three Gwenllians

'Heroine' was the word that Dad used to describe Gwenllian and I must say that another heroine still lives in Mynyddygarreg – Mari, my wife. She's in the same league as that princess, and has been a rock with all her support and motivation. And Manon (12 years old) and Gwenan (9), my two girls, are cast in the same mould – and have lifted my spirits with their honest and natural response to seeing their Dad without his right leg.

Musing

Back in Mynyddygarreg . . . I'm not walking yet but they've told me that I'll start taking a few steps in the near future. We have to keep faith. I can't emphasize enough what a big step it's been to come back home. A chance to shut my eyes and contemplate – I was raised in this cottage. We had a more primitive lifestyle then; we were self-sufficient, to a great extent. In the garden, we had specimens of nearly everything that grew, every vegetable and fruit under the sun – if you could eat it, it was there in Jac Gravell's garden! Dad could have had a food stall at Llanelli and Carmarthen markets. And Mam had her little border, full of pretty flowers, especially roses. Mam loved having roses in front of the house, which would give friends and visitors a royal welcome. I remember the first time I came up the hill to Brynhyfryd . . . I was about six years old. I remember seeing the windows and red door and falling in love with the place. The image is still there in my subconscious – I close my eyes and re-live the experience.

Despite living in a council house in the middle of Mynyddygarreg, Dad was desperate to return to his roots, a stone's throw from the mountain, and he had his way. Some of the father's genes have obviously been passed to the son, because I love coming home. The best part of any journey, after travelling to the four corners of earth, is the journey home – it's good to go away but coming back is even better.

Growing Back

I remember every hour of every day of the upbringing I had in Brynhyfryd – as it turned out, my childhood years laid solid foundations for the future. And talking about solid foundations – the village has been built on limestone, a stone that was vitally important for local industries – the tin works near the Gwendraeth Fach, the brick works in Kidwelly and Pedair Heol and Mynyddygarreg, the numerous quarries that attest to the great struggle of extracting the limestone, and the kilns, a part of the process to purify the lime.

I spent just over six weeks on my back at Glangwili Hospital – without a leg for the last fortnight. Still, I admit and recognize that what I went through was nothing compared to what some people have to suffer. I'm a lucky man – I have no reason to complain and I don't complain. I thank God and the specialist, the skilful surgeon, for saving my life. By now, every day is a bonus. I only just made it – I was within a day or two of losing my life. There's been an astounding change in my attitude towards life; I now appreciate breathing, I appreciate the fresh air, the wind and the rain. Every day, every second is precious.

What next? There's a long journey ahead. I hope that there will be many days, weeks, months and years to come but I'm ready for the challenge – I'm full of hope. The girls, Manon and Gwenan, have been amazing. When I was lying in bed (when both of them came to see Dad just before his big operation) Mari had to explain everything – she told them, plainly, that Dad was going to lose his leg. They were so mature; young perhaps, but also so intelligent, so honest and totally capable of taking in that awful news.

And the day after the operation, they breezed into the ward, but seemed more uncertain as they reached my bedside. I was lying on the bed, without a blanket over me; the left leg stretching down to the end of the bed, totally naturally, and the right one cut in half. I noticed Manon having a look over before planting a kiss on my lips. Then Gwenan, the picky one, doing exactly the same!

Mari's words broke the silence, 'Well, Manon, do you see anything odd? Is Dadi odd?' Her response was quick.

'He's always been a bit odd, hasn't he!'

Gwenan was more pensive:

'Mam, is Dad's leg going to grow back?' I cracked up laughing when I heard that. It lifted my spirits, there was a smile on my face, and my imagination was in overdrive. I looked down on my leg; I peeped on the six inch stump under the knee, with a big bandage around it, and challenged it, 'Go on, grow.' Now that would be a miracle! What would the specialists say if the leg grew back? I was tense and anxious before the three of them arrived, but in minutes we were all roaring with laughter around the bed, with our voices echoing around the ward.

The Urdd Eisteddfod, Carmarthenshire, May 2007

(Ray's first public appearance since his operation. His reaction was being filmed and recorded for the BBC programme, 'Sdim Cywilydd mewn Llefen (There's no shame in crying).

(In the bathroom)
This is the aftershave that Stephen Jones uses – Stephen is more handsome than me, but there we go! Right – shower, shave, brush my teeth; my clothes are downstairs.

(Ray is still in his wheelchair upstairs, and wheels himself to the top of the stairs)
This could be a problem but I'm familiar with the process. I have to be careful and move little by little out of the chair, in case I hit the stump. For the first fortnight, I slept downstairs but coming back upstairs was a huge psychological boost. I could then go into the bedroom, into the bathroom – and do the day-to-day things that we all do.

When Urdd Gobaith Cymru asked me to present the movement's talent prize at the end of the Carmarthenshire Eisteddfod, well hell, I could never refuse because we're talking about young people, the future!

(Downstairs, getting dressed)
I've already chosen the tie – my Owain Glyndŵr tie, my hero! I'm not sure which trousers to wear – long trousers or a pair of shorts? Mari suggested that shorts would be best. Is the tie alright?

The only places I visited after the operation were two hospitals – Glangwili and the Physiotherapy Department at Morriston. I didn't want to go anywhere else – I thought that people would be embarrassed. That's what worried me the most – making other people feel embarrassed.

(In the car on the way to Carmarthen. Sam, a little toy dog, is in Gwenan's arms).
'Is Sam sleeping, Gwenan?'
'Yes'.
'Sam has been all over the world – over to Australia, Spain, Kidwelly, Trimsaran, Ferryside. Has Sam been to Llansaint, Gwenan? And everywhere he goes, Gwenan, he says – Woof! Woof! Woof!'

(Dafydd Du's voice from the Eisteddfod stage)
'This year, the prize is going to be presented by a very, very special person.'

(A group of young people greet Ray and lead him to the stage).
If only I were about forty years younger!

(Dafydd Du's voice) 'Give a warm welcome to Ray Gravell.'

I hadn't really prepared myself for such a reaction. I'm not stupid, though; I knew that there would be some kind of reaction but everyone got on their feet at the same time . . . and I cried! It gave me a whole new lease of life.

(Asking Manon and Gwenan how the ceremony went)
You two are the best judges in the world. How did I do?

(Mari confirms that he did a good job by planting a great big kiss on his cheek – Sam's response was also complimentary).

Brynhyfryd's Happy Family.

The Wheels of Independence

David Gravell: 'Now then, Ray . . . I've got the key here, it's a card. Put the card in . . . use your left foot on the break and press the start button.

(Ray, carefully, steers the blue Renault Scenic towards the main road).

Ray: My God!

David: Are you comfortable there?

Ray: David, it's an amazing feeling. It's hard for me to express in words what kind of feeling it is. Oh, David! David! David! It's freedom, it's even a kind of independence.

David: It's the independence that's important. You're by yourself – you don't have to rely on anyone. You've got your car back.

Ray: David, I'm controlling it. I'm in control. And the car's moving perfectly – like a cat! Prrrrrrrrrrrrrrr!

Aunty Babs

(Ray speaks to the camera as he drives the new Renault Scenic). I'm on my way to the other end of the village to see Aunty Babs, my father's youngest sister. He had three sisters – Eileen, Olive and Barbara Jean. Unfortunately, there's only Babs left, the last of the line. She was ten years younger than my father. They lost their father, William Henry, when Babs was ten. We bought the house for her and her partner, Dennis. Babs has been good to me; to be honest, we've been good to each other. I love my Aunty Babs – I think the world of her. This is the first time that she's seen me driving since the operation.

The salt of the earth – Aunty Babs.

Ray: Aunty Babs!

Babs: How are you? *(Both hug each other; tears are flowing.)* Did you drive the car?

Ray: Of course. Less of those tears! What would your brother say?

Babs: A cup of tea, then.

Ray: Great! No one makes tea like Babs! *(Ray speaks to the camera while Babs prepares elevenses in the kitchen.)* She came down to see me in hospital – she shouldn't have. She struggles to walk after having operations on her hips – she's full of plastic! And then, she had to have a triple by-pass on her heart – I've only been through a tiny little thing compared to what Babs has been through, and what she's still going through. She's been a real inspiration to me, and she's just like my father. Thomas Jac Gravell could be fiery sometimes, but both of them were full of love and that's a family trait. *(Babs arrives with a teapot, crockery and a Teisen Lap)* I love you Babs!

Babs: And I love you Ray.

Ray: *(On the way out of Babs's drive)* Hell – I reverse better now than I did before the operation!

(There's no shame in Crying)

A word of advice to international referee Nigel Whitehouse, a former teammate from the mid-1980s.

The New Leg

(Ray and family are waiting patiently. The specialist is about to join them, with the new leg. Ray's eyes are shut).

Ray: I want to see the three of you react first of all. My eyes are still shut! *(Ray opens his eyes and sees the new leg).* Oh! Well! Well! Oh! Peter – *yr argol fawr*! It's like the shirt. I didn't realise the leg would be all scarlet. If it doesn't fit, I'll carry it with me. I'll be in the stand, waving it – Come on Scarlets! Well! Well! Peter bach! *(Ray turns to Manon and Gwenan)* What do you two think!

Manon and Gwenan: Cool!

Ray: I really didn't expect anything like this. I thought it would just look like a leg with a logo or something on it. I'm over the moon. Christmas has come early. I'll wear it with pride, everywhere. I won't hide this, Mari! Fantastic! It's different – it bends a bit. *(Manon is taking a photo).* Heavens above! *Angladd y marchog!*

Back in the Thick of It

I don't try to hide my disability – I show it with pride, hoping that it will help others. I have to slow down now – Mari gives me a lecture every day. Over the past month, I've been over-doing it a bit; going out at night, and the tiredness affects me. I'm back on my early-morning radio show and that's the main thing I want to do. I love the programme and I'm back in the thick of it. But I have to be careful and cut down on other things. But it's hard; every now and again, a charity gets in touch with me, or some charity representatives phone me, wanting me to help them out in some way or other. If I refuse the request, some think that I'm being a bit odd – but I'm starting to think that I'm going to have to disappoint some people, because I'm not the same as I used to be. I've got to think about that.

Fflur Dafydd performing live on *Rhaglen Grav* ('Grav's Show').

Two of Carmarthenshire's leading lights, poets Mererid Hopwood and Tudur Dylan Jones.

Well-wishers

Emotionally, I'm completely drained! Reading all the greetings that came to Brynhyfryd from all over the world, hundreds upon hundreds of them, brings back everything that's happened. It leaves me weak; emotionally, I'm as weak as a kitten. I don't like to read them in public, because they're very personal.

Llenwaf fy mhedair llinell â geiriau	(I fill my four lines with words
O gariad, i'th gymell.	Of love, to inspire you.
A mwy, Grav, rhof lond stafell	I'll give you, Grav, a roomful of love
I'th gael 'nôl yn hollol well.	To have you back, healthy and well.)

Mererid Hopwood

Phew! What can I say?

And here's Ceri Wyn Jones's verse – and he played for Wales. He was a centre, representing his country's secondary schools under eighteen (*This poem was presented to Grav at Stradey, the morning he began broadcasting again after his illness*):

Pan fo'r glaw yn curo'n drwm	(When the rain keeps falling down
A rhaglenni'r radio'n llwm,	When the radio makes us frown
Yr un gân yw'n cais ni i gyd –	We have only one request –
O na fyddai'n Grav o hyd.	We want Grav 'cause West is Best.)

Oh! Ceri bach! And if I read Dic's poem I'd be crying murders. They're personal and I know that Manon and Gwenan will, after my days, treasure them and they'll understand the significance of the words.

And some evenings, I come into this room, read them quietly and cry. Some of the strongest men I know, some of the bravest men I know, cry. So, there's no shame in crying. Oh no! Not at all!

(There's no shame in Crying)

Fair Play to the Ospreys

The regional teams – the Dragons, the Blues, the Ospreys (and the Scarlets of course) are amazing. Believe you me, there's respect and camaraderie between them, and I should know as I spend every game on the sidelines for *Y Clwb Rygbi* on S4C. During the game, there's a belligerent spirit – when I played for Llanelli against Swansea, Neath, Cardiff, Newport and Aberavon, there were fierce battles and frayed tempers; as a player, it wasn't that I wanted to kill my opponent – but on the other hand, perhaps I did want to kill him – it was very intense and aggressive. And then, it's the end of the game, the final whistle, and after the rivalry, the socialising starts – the friendship is genuine and that's one

Receiving Stradey's acclamation at the testimonial match against Bath, August 2007.

thing I've carried with me from the last century to the present. And the Ospreys, of all teams, also toe the line – we did a broadcast recently from Ysgol Tirdeunaw in Swansea. I had loads of cards and messages from schools in west Wales; classes and pupils sent very personal messages, and one of them really tickled me. It was from Thomas Maggs, and at the time he was a pupil in his final year at Ysgol Gynradd Gymraeg Tirdeunaw. Thomas's card came with a bundle of cards from the school. He'd portrayed me in the school's *Cân Actol* [short musical] for the Urdd Eisteddfod – Grav was the main character and he did a decent job of it – better than I would have done myself:

'Welcome to Grav's radio programme – with you every morning from west Wales – West is best.'

This is what Thomas wrote in his card, in Welsh:

Thomas Maggs (now a pupil at Swansea's first Welsh-medium comprehensive, Ysgol Gyfun Bryntawe.)

GET WELL SOON GRAV –
YOU ARE MY HERO
BUT I STILL HATE THE
SCARLETS!

Thomas's greeting really lifted my spirits, fair play; there was real honesty in the message.

Gwenan

(On the beach in Borth with Gwenan, October 2007 – staying for the weekend with John Hefin and Elin).

Gwenan, you've found a stone with a hole in it . . . according to the old Celts, a stone like that brings luck to people, and as we're descended from the Celts, it's bound to bring you luck. Don't lose it! You found it, Gwenan; you should keep it.

Manon

(Ray is quiet for once, listening to Manon speaking to the camera, while they were filming a BBC documentary programme).

The latest experience hasn't changed him at all. In the past, he used to complain. When his foot hurt, he complained. He still moans all the time, the same as he's always done since I was born! So nothing's changed really. Still the same old Dad!

Gwenan, Manon and me with Sydney Harbour Bridge behind us.

Happy Birthday

Ray: *(Ray opens the present – Mari and the girls wait for his reaction).* A wallet! Just what Dad wanted! The smell of the leather is lovely. I'm very pleased with this. Spot on!

Manon: *(reading the label).* Bio-degradable!

Ray: There we go! If we don't have money to buy food, I can eat the wallet! It's great to be here. *(Ray cries quietly)* Tears of joy. Fifty-six years old! Fifty six not out, and there are more runs yet to come! *Iechyd da*! This old world is an exciting journey and we don't know what's ahead of us. We've got to take each day as it comes!

7

'By God . . .'

I used to sing Dafydd Iwan songs before every game, and drew comfort and strength from letting rip in the changing room at Stradey, at international venues and on buses en route to meeting the enemy. No doubt it was a nervous reaction to help bolster my confidence, and thanks to Dafydd's melodies, much of the uncertainty was indeed dispelled. Dafydd actually visited me in hospital in the middle of his frenzied canvassing on behalf of Plaid Cymru's election campaign. He found – or he made – the time.

I'll never forget, seven years ago at the time of the Llanelli National Eisteddfod (and that's what I call an eisteddfod!). A concert was organised in the main pavilion and Dafydd asked me to introduce him to the audience – the place was packed, and I reminded him that he had, some years ago, made me a promise. Which ever of us would be first to go, the first to cross the bar, that is – if I went before him, he would sing '*Myn Duw, mi wn y daw*' in my funeral. I said this with a liberal helping of humour. Of all his songs, this is my favourite; it's a song that tells of Owain Glyndŵr.

When he walked into the ward in Glangwili Hospital, Carmarthen, as I lay in bed, I saw him at once in front of me. And I thought – Damn; how close he had come to singing '*Myn Duw*' . . . not in hospital that afternoon, but in Horeb Chapel, Mynyddygarreg.

BY GOD, I KNOW HE WILL COME!

The blood of all the warriors that flowed onto the grass
Was long ago deleted by the rain,
I can't hear for the sound of thunder, I can't see for the lightning's flash,
The despair is a constant dark refrain.
O, where is Owain today? O, where is Owain now?

The tide will turn again, the rainbow follows rain,
And after night, I know the dawn will break.

I know that Owain will return,
I know that Owain will return:
As the tide will turn again, and the rainbow follows rain,
As dawn will follow night,
By God, I know he'll come,
By God, I know he'll come.

The battle was not futile, the bloodshed was not in vain,
There's still the sound of victory in the air:
I hear the soldiers' voices, I hear their marching feet,
Walking from Snowdonia mountains fair:

Let's cast aside our fears, and all our nagging doubts,
Owain's ready once again to lead the way,
From his refuge in Eryri, he will lead his loyal troops
To herald the free Wales at break of day.
By God, I know he will come!
By God, I know he will come!

(*Translation of* 'Myn Duw, mi wn y daw' *by Dafydd Iwan – Cyhoeddiadau Sain.*)

Ray Gravell's Career 1951 – 2007

1951: Arrive in the Gwendraeth valley on September 12 (sharing a birthday with Delme Thomas).

1955: Education calling, and Mynyddygarreg Primary School faces a challenge and a half.

1963: Fail the 11+ (ball games to blame!) and a journey along the A484 to Burry Port Secondary School.

1966: Heroic effort in the classroom – Carmarthen Grammar School agrees to educate the boy from Mynyddygarreg.

1968: The first red shirt – representing Wales Youth against France in Figeac.

1970: The first Scarlet shirt – a friendly against Lampeter on April 30.

1972: The youngest member of the Scarlets team to face the mighty All Blacks at Stradey. Llanelli 9 New Zealand 3.

1975: Realise a dream (Dad's and mine). First cap for Wales in the cauldron at Parc des Princes. Six new caps, but Wales, contrary to expectation, smash the *Tricolores*.

1975: Acquire posh accent! Chosen to represent the Baa-baas.

1976: Grand Slam under the captaincy of Mervyn Davies.

1978: Freezing cold, Wales shine against Scotland and Ray Gravell scores his first international try. Tip top! Another Grand Slam season.

1980: Captain of Llanelli. Wow! Lead the club for two seasons.

1980: From Brynhyfryd to the Veldt! Included in the Lions squad for the South Africa tour. Played in all four tests.

1983: First broadcasting experience: presenting *Teulu Ffôn* – HTV's family quiz on S4C.

1985: My last game for the Scarlets, on January 26, in the cup against Llandovery – 485 games, 120 tries.

1985: Behind the microphone! Summarizing with Huw Llywelyn Davies on S4C, and plenty of exposure on BBC Radio Cymru on Saturday afternoons.

1985: Plenty of work! A leading role in 'Bonner' on S4C.

1988: Working with Frank Hennessy on the popular programme *Street Life* and later *I'll Show You Mine*.

1991: *Filipina Dreamgirls* – Bill Maynard, Charlie Drake and me!

1991: Mari and I were married in Horeb Chapel, Mynyddygarreg.

1992: A role in *Rebecca's Daughters* with Peter O'Toole, Paul Rhys, Joely Richardson and Dafydd Hywel.

1992: Another role! This time in the film *Damage* directed by Louis Malle. A distinguished cast, including Jeremy Irons, Juliette Binoche, and Miranda Richardson.

1995: Manon born, July 6

1997: An incredible honour: invested as the Gorsedd's Sword Bearer.

1998: Gwenan born, July 22nd.

1998: Elected President of Llanelli Rugby Football Club.

2005: Broadcasting on the Grand Slam; the first since 1978. An unforgettable experience.

Terry Morris's comic cartoon.